JOHNNY
The
Pas
Depp

Stone Wallace

ICON
PRESS

First printed in 2004 10 9 8 7 6 5 4 3 2 1

Printed in Canada

The Publisher: Icon Press, an imprint of Folklore Publishing

Website: www.folklorepublishing.com

Library and Archives Canada Cataloguing in Publication

Wallace, Stone, 1957–
  Johnny Depp : the passionate rebel / Stone Wallace.

(Star biographies)
Includes bibliographical references.
ISBN 1-894864-17-4

  1. Depp, Johnny. 2. Motion picture actors and actresses—
United States—Biography. I. Title. II. Series.

PN2287.D447W34 2005   791.4302'8'092   C2004-907060-6

Project Director: Faye Boer
Editorial: Faye Boer, Nicholle Carrière
Layout & Production: Trina Koscielnuk
Cover Design: Valentino
Book Design: Anne & Dion

Cover Image: Courtesy of Steven Granitz/WireImage.com

Photography credits: Every effort has been made to accurately credit the sources of photo-graphs. Any errors or omissions should be directed to the publisher for changes in future editions. Photographs courtesy of International Communication Systems.

We acknowledge the support of the Alberta Foundation for the Arts for our publishing program.

PC:P6

Alberta Foundation for the Arts

Table of Contents

Dedication

This book is dedicated with affection and appreciation to two special friends, Philip Chamberlin and Dolores Fuller

Acknowledgements

Most sincere thanks to Dr. Philip Chamberlin and Dolores Fuller for all their support and knowledge concerning the topic. A special thank you to Thomas Fuller for his technical know-how and support. And as always, a special thank you to Faye Boer of Folklore Publishing for her consistent understanding and support and belief in the project and the author.

Foreword

*Johnny, Johnny,
burning bright
In the forests of
the night!*

When Johnny Depp's character in Jim Jarmusch's neglected 1995 masterpiece *Dead Man* is introduced as "William Blake," this paraphrase by the great British poet leaped into my mind. Johnny Depp burns brightly in the contemporary cinematic jungle, the fearful symmetry of this talent outrunning the vehicles that have carried him to the high place he holds today. I was asked by the author of this book to help introduce the pages you are about to read because I was once in love with Ed Wood, whose character Johnny played 10 years ago in the second film in which Johnny acted with his friend and discoverer, Tim Burton. Alas, I have never met Johnny, so my remarks come

Ah, but Johnny! He nailed Eddie's passion to make movies, his immense joy in his work and his understanding that what counts is the "big picture," not the tiny details.

from a distance that some may think disqualifies me to comment. But I make bold to speak because my understanding and respect for Eddie gives me a perspective on Johnny's performance in *Ed Wood* that I believe overcomes the disadvantage of not knowing Johnny personally. But I know his work, and after all, an artist *is* ultimately his work, is he not?

When Disney sent a limo to carry me to the premiere of *Ed Wood* in Hollywood, I was admittedly filled with trepidation. Why? Because I had read the script and felt it untrue to the three principal characters: Eddie, Bela (Lugosi) and me. Certainly Eddie was not the joke dreamed up by the Medved brothers to sell their books highlighting the worst in cinematic achievement. Eddie passionately aspired to make movies. Unfortunately, his sensibilities ran to low budget Westerns, crime stories and horror films, as I belatedly came to realize. But against all odds Eddie got five films made in a 10-year period—the identical achievement Orson Welles accomplished in the same

10-year period with the advantage of extraordinary talent. Bela Lugosi was a sophisticated aristocratic gentleman, not the foul-mouthed drug addict invented by the talented scriptwriters whose absence of research was overcome by Martin Landau's brilliant delivery of their lines. It is best here that I overlook the mannered reading that Sarah "Jurassic" Parker gave to the lines she was handed, except to say that she lacked sufficient talent or imagination to make something of the part. She was an insult to me, and I only find comfort in the fact that her role was so forgettable it can do me no lasting damage.

Ah, but Johnny! He nailed Eddie's passion to make movies, his immense joy in his work and his understanding that what counts is the "big picture," not the tiny details. Also, I should add, he truly expressed Eddie's love for our dear friend Bela Lugosi and the respect one should have for a talented veteran actor, in this case for one no longer in demand. This was the movie's heart, and it won me over completely.

Johnny, Johnny, burning bright
In the forests of the night!

Of course, I was already a Johnny Depp fan since a couple of the *21 Jump Street* episodes, and especially since Tim Burton's wonderful *Edward Scissorhands* and *What's Eating Gilbert Grape*, so how could I resist Johnny as Eddie? The very next year after *Ed Wood*, Johnny astonished me again by dominating scenes with the indominable Marlon Brando in *Don Juan de Marco*, then with Al Pacino in *Donnie Brasco*. He carried *Dead Man* by himself, although it had a remarkable cast that included John Hurt, Billy Bob Thornton and, in his last role, Robert Mitchum. We have now seen *Pirates of the Caribbean*, which again showcases Johnny's consummate ability to imbue his roles with surprisingly original twists that have broadened his public appeal. Still, Johnny has not yet found the script that will give full scope to his talent. His personal masterwork remains to be made. When it finally comes, I'll be waiting…along with the growing legion of his fans.

–Dolores Fuller, May 2004

In Step With Depp

Let me confess at the outset that I am an enormous admirer of Johnny Depp's work, although prior to beginning research on this project, I realized that I really hadn't seen many of his films. How then could I appreciate and critique the talents of a man whose screen performances I'd actually viewed could truthfully be counted on the fingers of one hand?

I suppose I could best answer that question by issuing a challenge to those who enjoy observing and examining the qualities of fine screen acting. Watch a Johnny Depp movie and see how soon you can forget the experience.

Johnny Depp is intriguing. Perhaps to some he is an acquired taste. But like the sampling of fine food, invariably he leaves you wanting more.

And when the accomplishments of today's top movie talents are examined and discussed by future film scholars, Johnny Depp's name will be high on the list.

He has been described by many of his colleagues as a contemporary James Dean. He is also one of the most eclectic, eccentric and overall individual actors ever to reach the heights of superstardom. Certainly, Brando, Dean and Montgomery Clift paved the road before him. But Johnny's movie success was preceded with a distinct disadvantage—he first achieved fame as a TV star. Yet he emerged from this "chew 'em up and spit 'em out" meat grinder to both survive and flourish, joining only a few others who have enjoyed this distinction, chiefly Robin Williams, Bruce Willis and Michael J. Fox. Furthermore, Johnny escaped his "pin-up" image and avoided the post-teenybopper career pitfalls experienced by David Cassidy and Kirk Cameron, among others, to earn respect in his own right as a highly respected, serious film actor—admired by critics and audiences alike—even if some of the projects he chose were risky at best.

Pirates of the Caribbean: The Curse of the Black Pearl (2003)

But this is how Johnny chose to play the game: against the odds. He gained a reputation for turning down big-budget, high-profile studio roles that would heighten his burgeoning stardom to attach his name value to smaller, more personal projects whose characters and stories (along with the creative talent involved) he felt an affinity for.

Most of Johnny's choices have been based on artistic preferences, often sacrificing the mainstream for the abstract. Of course, he is not averse to appearing in a Hollywood commercial blockbuster, but his number one consideration in choosing a role is that he must find the part both personally and professionally satisfying.

Perhaps that is the secret behind Johnny Depp's success. He is not afraid to take chances as an actor. While some multi-million-dollar film players refuse to stray too far from their established image, Johnny again proves a unique exception. Most probably because Johnny has never allowed himself to be locked into an audience-proof character.

And Johnny always delivers. He never cheats by merely "walking through" a part. He always surprises and clearly enjoys challenging his own acting abilities as much as providing entertainment for the audience.

Contemporary moviegoers crave escapism, and box office receipts prove the ongoing popularity of superheroes (Arnold Schwarzenegger) or the average Joe suddenly thrust into a superhero-like situation, where against all the odds, he or she not only survives but emerges triumphant (Bruce Willis). Johnny Depp, too, has ventured into this realm, but he refuses to be cast as an invincible action hero. He insists that his "heroes" come equipped with identifiable human foibles and frailities.

Cry-Baby (1990)

Are these characteristics of Johnny Depp, the man? Definitely. Loner, misfit, eccentric, romantic, rebel, perhaps even a touch delicate and dandified. The complexities of Johnny's personality have all found their way into his various screen portrayals. And revealing these inherent quirks and attributes is a bold decision and major undertaking for a man who prefers to keep his private life insulated from public scrutiny.

To that end, Johnny reveals very little about himself when discussing his latest film project. He understands that publicity is a peripheral yet vital part of the business that has made him rich and famous. He openly, often eagerly, responds to questions about the preparation for a role with perceptive comments about the story, the director and his co-stars. But Johnny's inherent politeness can be challenged when journalists try to segue professional conversation into questions regarding his often-controversial personal life. Perhaps Johnny's reticence is not so difficult to understand. Movie stardom is not an ambition he had ever actively sought. He appreciates the accolades and the financial rewards, not to mention the artistic challenge his various film roles provide, but he hadn't spent a lifetime, or even half of his current lifetime dreaming of cinematic glory.

The good fortune that embraced Johnny Depp occurred through circumstances not of his own making, and even once he achieved professional success, the reluctant actor refused to capitulate to the apparent and transparent seduction of celebrity.

Johnny Depp, however, is an unquestioned megastar. While his box office flops have for the most part outweighed his financial triumphs, he remains consistently in demand by major Hollywood studios and top-line independent producers. And with the commercial and critical acclaim of *Pirates of the Caribbean*, it looks as if Johnny has finally scored an equal success with both reviewers and the popcorn-buying public.

One can only imagine what film challenges await Johnny Depp in this new millennium. In just over 20 years, he's already played an incredible variety of roles, ranging from a lonely, abandoned laboratory creation to a troubled yet always-enthusiastic trans-vestite Z-film director to the least Errol–Flynn-like pirate ever to sail the seven seas. Perhaps, on the surface, Johnny Depp's film resume reads like a catalog of crazies, yet it is through his talent for creative expression and inner exploration that Johnny has paid forward his gift for characterization by allowing audiences to recognize and honor their own unique individuality.

Growing Up Johnny

O n looking back at his roots, perhaps it is not difficult to understand Johnny Depp's leaning towards eccentric and offbeat movie roles. His was certainly not a traditional childhood upbringing.

He entered the world as John Christopher Depp II on June 9, 1963, under the astrological sign of Gemini, the twins, the duality of which would hold particular relevance for Johnny in his professional career. His place of birth, on the other hand, marked no such significance for the future movie star. Owensboro, Kentucky held no greater claim to fame than its annual hosting of the International Bar-B-Q Festival, hence its reputation as the "barbecue capital of the world."

...it is not difficult to understand Johnny Depp's leaning towards eccentric and offbeat movie roles.

This title alone suggests a complacent middle-class lifestyle at odds with the rebel Johnny would become.

Johnny was the fourth of four children, preceded by sisters Debbie and Christine and stepbrother Danny from his mother Betty Sue's first marriage. Johnny's father, John Sr., was employed as a city engineer, but his wages were not sufficient to adequately provide for his family, so Betty Sue worked as a waitress at a local coffeehouse.

Johnny's ethnic background is a mixture of Irish and German, but he has always been most proud of his Native American ancestry on his mother's side. As a boy, Johnny always felt a special bond with his grandfather who was a full-blooded Cherokee. Johnny affectionately referred to his grandfather as PawPaw. While never particularly vain about his looks, Johnny was proud of the striking chiseled features accentuated by sharp cheekbones that he'd inherited from PawPaw. Yet more importantly, it was with his grandfather's influence that he adopted a strong, unwavering emotional connection to his heritage.

Boyhood friends would later remember Johnny insisting on playing "the Indian" in backyard Cowboys and Indian adventures, where Johnny would frequently frustrate his playmates by refusing to die when shot with pretend bullets.

While Johnny had a close relationship with his parents (particularly his mother), his special memories were the times he spent with PawPaw. Johnny enjoyed those carefree days when he and his grandfather picked tobacco together or just shared quiet conversations where Johnny learned more about his proud Native heritage. And although PawPaw lived to the ripe old age of 102, his death in 1970 was a terrible blow to Johnny.

> "But somehow I believe that he's still around," Johnny said years later. "Guiding, watching. I have close calls sometimes, and I think 'How did I get out of that?' I've just got a feeling that it's PawPaw looking out for me."

Johnny was just seven when the family moved from Kentucky south to the working-class community of Miramar, Florida. There his father hoped to find more lucrative employment, but while John Sr. actively sought out job opportunities, his family lived in a motel for almost a year. This was one of many such episodes that would later cause Johnny to remember his childhood as a nomadic existence.

"I don't even have a mental picture of the houses we lived in because there were so many," he said.

Fortune finally seemed to smile upon the Depp clan when John Sr. finally found work as Director of Public Works at Miramar. The family celebrated by purchasing a house and settling into a comfortable suburban routine.

Johnny was glad to final have the stability of a permanent home, but because of the family's frequent moves, it was difficult for him to make friends easily and blend into an accepted school and social life.

"That was tough," Johnny admitted. "It got to the point where I wouldn't bother to introduce myself to kids in the new neighborhood where we'd moved because I knew I wouldn't be around long enough to really get to know them."

Johnny felt isolated, or as he later described it, "Like I was a total freak." The only closeness he ever felt was with his family, and to this day he remains a strong advocate of the family unit.

"Let's face it, without family, you have nothing. It's the most important thing in the world."

Although some aspects of Johnny's later image may seem at odds with this statement, he has proved his sincerity by generously sharing his success with his siblings, not through charity, but by a genuine appreciation of their talents and his reliance on them. Brother Dan later co-wrote a movie script with Johnny, and his sister, Christi, has proved herself invaluable in organizing Johnny's hectic work schedule.

Life in Miramar quickly grew stagnant for Johnny. It was a working-class community that offered little stimulation for a boy whose imagination had already surpassed his years. Johnny harbored fantasies of becoming the next Evel Knievel, Bruce Lee or the first white player on the Harlem Globetrotters basketball team.

Instead, he quickly fell into a boring middle-class existence that was further emphasized when his father suggested he try out for the high school football team. Johnny complied, but quickly withdrew when he discovered he had no real interest in or aptitude for the sport.

"Let's face it, without family, you have nothing. It's the most important thing in the world."

To alleviate his restlessness, Johnny adopted a punk image and began hanging out with a rough crowd, participating in burglaries and school vandalism. He and his pals broke into schools after dark and randomly selected classrooms that they'd thoroughly trash without fear of the consequences. He also began shoplifting.

In later years, Johnny would say that he never personally pursued these endeavors with malicious intent, explaining, "I was curious."

Johnny was curious about other matters as well. At age 13, he'd already experienced his first sexual encounter with a girl four years his senior. And he had experimented with drugs, ranging from weed to hard hallucinogens. Although Johnny claims he gave up narcotics at 14 when he realized where that path would lead him, his two other vices, alcohol and tobacco, have remained somewhat more difficult habits to break. Tobacco in particular has been a stubborn addiction, to the point where Johnny once remarked on television that he wished his face came equipped with two mouths so that he could "double the pleasure."

Johnny credits his brother Dan with setting him back on the right road. Dan had given Johnny a copy of the book *On the Road* by Jack Kerouac. Johnny immediately embraced the novel, claiming that its text has helped him weather the turmoil he's endured throughout both his personal and professional life.

"Kerouac's book is like the Koran to me," Johnny once explained.

Yet while Johnny was trying to move forward in a positive direction, he was suddenly faced with the most traumatic event a child can experience. Ongoing strains in John Sr. and Betty Sue's marriage finally brought the couple to divorce. The breakup was a severe blow to Johnny who, although he remembered difficult times around the house, refused to choose sides and remained

17

close to both parents. He did, however, decide to live with his mother.

At the time of the split, Johnny was the only one of the children still living at home (his sister Debbie had moved in with her father). Fortunately, the bond between the siblings remained strong, so that when things got rough, Johnny could lean on his older brother and sisters.

> While trying to deal with his own despair, Johnny was troubled to witness the physical and emotional toll the divorce took on his mother. He tried to suppress his own troubled feelings to help her through the difficult period.

Johnny's schooling also suffered as a result of the breakup. He'd never really excelled at academics; his school record was peppered with colorful accounts of truancy and misconduct—one of his frequent suspensions came when he mooned his gym teacher. Although Johnny possessed an intelligent, inquisitive and imaginative mind, the regimen of the classroom simply bored him. In 1979, at age 16, he finally dropped out of school.

Perhaps as a way of coping with his troubles, and maybe his own feelings of guilt, Johnny began experimenting with self-scarring. This is a practice that he engages in from time to time, explaining, "In a way your body is a journal, and the scars are sort of entries in it."

His best friend, Sal Jenco, had also seen his own parents recently divorce. Sal decided to move out on his own and had no place to go, so he lived in his '67 Impala. Johnny felt sorry for his friend and moved in with him. The two boys shared the bizarre, cramped living arrangement while subsisting on beer and submarine sandwiches stolen from 7-Eleven stores.

Johnny really had no idea what he was going to do with his life. He had no high school diploma and no trade. He began to suffer

anxiety attacks at the thought of ending up a loser, and if not unemployed, then working at a gas station for the rest of his life.

Johnny saw just one ray of hope, though the light it provided for a professional future was dim.

Johnny had had a passion for music since his early days in Owensboro when he attended the revival meetings led by his uncle, who was a fundamentalist minister. Johnny remembered that when this man preached fire-and-brimstone sermons, the congregation literally fell at his feet seeking redemption for their sins—Johnny just sat mesmerized by the gospel music.

Although Johnny wouldn't realize it for years to come, he benefited even more from these tent services, gleaning the power of performance, as he recalled the preacher's fiery pronouncements that held his followers spellbound.

At the time, Johnny had no acting ambitions. His main interest was music. When he was 12, his mother bought him his first electric guitar for $25. Johnny locked himself away in his room for hours, neglecting school assignments to master the chords of his musical heroes.

Eventually, Johnny felt confident enough to form his own garage rock band, Flame. He modeled the group on the high-energy bands popular at the time, fashioning outrageous outfits for its members with borrowed apparel from his mother's closet.

As a high-school dropout with no other skills to draw on, Johnny decided to embrace his musical ambitions with complete focus and determination. His youthful enthusiasm refused to let him contemplate the possibility of failure. He knew the road ahead would be difficult, but it was his one, perhaps his only, chance to make something out of his life.

Flame evolved into a new band called The Kids, and the other members were as serious as Johnny in their intent. They began getting gigs at local bars, but unfortunately, Johnny was under-age. Having generally hustled their way into these commitments, the band further relied on chutzpah to work out a solution regarding Johnny's age. He entered the club through the back entrance, then left after the first set. Perhaps not a glamorous beginning for a dreamy-eyed rock star, but Johnny hung in there, ignoring the humiliation of secretive entrances and exits, collecting his pocket pay of $25 per night, thrilled to be making a buck by pursuing his passion.

The Kids' high-energy rock stylings quickly gained them a local reputation, and the band found themselves opening for such popular groups as the B52s and Talking Heads. Their earnings increased considerably to sometimes over $2000. Eventually, they opened for Iggy Pop, and the experience would remain a particularly embarrassing episode for Johnny.

As the story goes, Johnny and his band went to a nearby bar to unwind following their opening for the concert. For whatever reason, Johnny proceeded to get completely drunk, and when Iggy walked into the bar, Johnny began spewing insults and obscenities at

> His youthful enthusiasm refused to let him contemplate the possibility of failure. He knew the road ahead would be difficult, but it was his one, perhaps his only, chance to make something out of his life.

him. Instead of lowering himself to Johnny's intoxicated level and making a scene, Iggy calmly approached Johnny and responded to his foul remarks by calling him "a little turd." He then turned and walked away, leaving a barely comprehending Johnny looking like a fool.

Johnny was at a loss to explain why he'd acted so disgracefully towards a man he genuinely admired. Of course, it was the drinking, but perhaps, inebriated, Johnny was also gloating over the success his own band was enjoying fronting for such acts as Iggy Pop. The incident bothered Johnny for a long time afterwards.

Fortunately, a few years later, when Johnny was enjoying his first taste of movie success in the film **Cry-Baby**, Iggy Pop also had a role in the John Waters production. The two warily discussed the incident, with Johnny apologizing for his drunken behavior and Iggy graciously admitting, "I was probably in the same condition as you, maybe worse." A long-term friendship instantly solidified.

Outside of such booze-fueled incidents, Johnny and his band continued to enjoy some success as a Florida bar band.

Then fate stepped in.

chapter 2

Lori Anne
And L.A.

i n 1983, while The Kids were experiencing career ups and downs, Johnny was introduced to 25-year-old Lori Anne Allison, herself an aspiring musician and sister of one of the band members. The two were immediately attracted to one another and were married within two months.

With responsibilities as a husband now upon him, Johnny made the decision that The Kids should expand their horizons and consider moving to Los Angeles, where, perhaps with typical enthusiastic naïveté, he believed they could secure a recording deal. The other band members agreed, and so with stars glistening in their eyes, they headed for Hollywood…where they immediately discovered a brutal truth. While The Kids had modest success in Florida, in Tinseltown, the band was just one of hundreds of hopefuls looking to achieve fame and fortune based on their local reputation.

Such competition proved discouraging for the band, but Johnny and the others refused to accept defeat. The only concession they made to the situation was to take menial jobs to survive—a low point in Johnny's life. He was forced to capitulate to his lack of education by working at a variety of low-paying, brain-deadening jobs. He worked as a telemarketer with a sleazy company where he sold substandard merchandise to customers.

"I got a hundred bucks a week for ripping people off," was how Johnny described this job.

Later, he acquired more reputable, but equally unsatisfying employment, selling personalized pens to companies over the phone. In a good week, he might bring home $100.

Johnny was discouraged, but the one thing that kept him going was making a success of his band. The group considered that maybe their name was too simplistic, not identifiable enough. They decided to rename The Kids with a label that had more impact: Six Gun Method.

Perhaps this trading of monikers had the desired effect because they were soon hired for a few gigs and even opened for Billy Idol. Despite such heady successes, the work was not steady, and tensions grew among the members.

Strain was also beginning to show in Johnny's marriage to Lori Anne. Both realized that they had married young—Johnny was five years Lori Anne's junior—and that starry-eyed romantic idealism does not make for a lasting marital union. After two years together, the couple realized they were moving in different directions—Johnny still intent on pursuing his musical dreams and Lori Anne wanting stability.

Theirs was not an acrimonious divorce. They remained friends, and through their ongoing friendship, Johnny was introduced to the person who would change his career focus and set him on his path to cinematic destiny.

Lori Anne had secured employment as a makeup artist, and one of the aspiring young actors she had come to know through her work was a fellow named Nicolas Coppola. Later to achieve international movie fame as Nicolas Cage, Nic Coppola was a struggling yet serious actor with strong family ties to the movie industry. His uncle was the legendary director of *The Godfather* films, Francis Ford Coppola, and Nic's aunt was the respected actress, Talia Shire, perhaps best known for her role as Adrian in the *Rocky* series.

Lori Anne and Nic dated for a while, and on occasion Johnny joined them for drinks. Nic and Johnny became friends, and

Johnny soon moved into Nic's apartment near Hollywood Boulevard, where he confessed to helping himself to his friend's Mexican coins, which he'd exchange so he could purchase hot dogs or cigarettes.

It was Nic who suggested that Johnny give acting a try. Johnny had never even considered becoming an actor; he still had his sights set on a successful music career. However, as Nic explained it, both acting and playing music were performing. His arguments finally persuaded Johnny, and he agreed to meet with Nic's agent, Tracey Jacobs.

Tracey saw potential in Johnny—a shy yet appealing talent. She also liked his look, although Johnny's appearance was scruffy, as if the rebel in him was saying: "This is who I am. Take it or leave it." Perhaps Tracey was impressed that he wasn't trying to impress her. In any event, Tracey set up an audition for Johnny for a horror movie.

Wes Craven is a former-academic-turned-filmmaker who specializes in the horror genre. His breakthrough movie, *The Hills Have Eyes*, was a rather unpleasant tale about a family of campers besieged by a family of mutated cannibals. The success of this movie prompted Craven to continue in the genre, and among his many credits are *Deadly Blessing, Deadly Friend, Swamp Thing* and *Vampire in Brooklyn* starring Eddie Murphy. *A Nightmare on Elm Street* was Craven's attempt to create a new monster, thrusting the traditional bogeyman into a not-so-traditional setting: the creature stalks its victims through their dreams while they are asleep.

Tracey saw potential in Johnny—a shy yet appealing talent. She also liked his look, although Johnny's appearance was scruffy, as if the rebel in him was saying: "This is who I am. Take it or leave it."

Johnny was up for the role of Glen Lantz, the teen heroine's boyfriend. Immediately, he knew he was wrong for the part. As presented in the script, the character was a big, blond surfer jock. As Johnny described himself at the time: "I was this scrawny guy with spiky hair and earrings who looked as if he'd never been on a beach in his life." Still, Johnny worked hard preparing for his audition, staying up for two nights running lines with a friend.

Craven's project was geared towards teenage audiences, so Craven brought along his own adolescent daughter to read lines with the auditioning actors. It was she who invariably made the casting choice concerning Glen Lantz.

"I thought Johnny was good," Craven said later. "But after he was through, my daughter couldn't stop talking about how 'hot' he was and what a 'fox' he was. Her response was so overwhelming that I felt I had to go along with her decision, hoping that what she obviously saw in the guy would be noticed by other teenage girls, as well."

A Nightmare on Elm Street was released November 16, 1984, and was an immediate box office hit. Its success has spawned seven sequels so far. The main star of the film, of course, is Freddy Kruger, played by the amazingly versatile Robert Englund. Freddy Kruger truly is the stuff of nightmares, a psychopathic child murderer put to a fiery death by outraged parents after the law proves powerless to punish him. He returns from death as a hideously scarred demon complete with a knife-fingered glove, who torments, terrorizes and ultimately kills the new generation of Elm Street children while they are asleep and at their most vulnerable.

As the body count rises and the adults refuse to acknowledge this "urban legend," the surviving teenagers led by Nancy (Heather Langenkamp) decide to fight Freddy on his own turf. But it's already too late for Johnny's character because Glen drifted off to sleep while talking to Nancy on the telephone, only to be ingested whole headfirst and regurgitated as a bloody fountain.

> "I thought Johnny was good," Craven said later. "But after he was through, my daughter couldn't stop talking about how 'hot' he was and what a 'fox' he was."

While not the critics' favorite, *A Nightmare on Elm Street* was an enormous box office smash, eventually grossing $25,504,000. Johnny was thrilled to be paid $1200 per week for six weeks' work.

Craven later said of Johnny that, while he was inexperienced, he picked up the process of film acting quite quickly and was eager to learn. Johnny had no illusions about instant stardom—his most memorable scene was performed by 100 gallons of fake blood.

"What kind of reviews could I expect?" Johnny said with a shrug. "Johnny Depp was great as the kid who died?"

Johnny had survived and also rather enjoyed his first exposure to movie work. But he didn't look at acting as anything more than a well-paying day job that he did while waiting to resume his music career. It was only after the band broke up for good that he decided to pursue acting as a full-time career. After all, he wasn't about to return to telemarketing.

His agent secured other auditions for Johnny based on the success of the Craven film. He appeared in some television shows before landing his next screen role. Sadly, whatever momentum he'd gained with *Nightmare* came to a screeching halt with *Private Resort*. A lame teen sex comedy, the movie is notable only for its casting of Johnny and two other up-and-comers: Rob Morrow (soon to achieve small-screen fame on *Northern Exposure*) and bad-boy comic Andrew Dice Clay.

The 1985 movie was filmed in Florida, which allowed for a pleasant homecoming of sorts, but overall, the film was a disappointing experience for Johnny. He played Jack, who along with his buddy Ben (Morrow), checks into a Florida resort to score with the local girls. Various predictable complications ensue, and the whole affair descends into slapdash slapstick, not even meeting the artistic heights of Larry, Curly and Moe. The movie's single point of interest, which remains to this day, is a brief shot of a nude Johnny that occurs about 15 minutes into the picture.

Regarding *Private Resort,* Johnny said, "I wasn't embarrassed by it, especially as I didn't think I was going to be an actor. I was just trying to make some money. I still considered myself a musician."

In 1986, Johnny appeared in the TV movie *Slow Burn.* Johnny was pleased to be acting in a crime thriller rather than another moronic sophomore comedy, and especially one with an impressive pedigree. The movie was based on the critically acclaimed novel *Castles Burning* by Arthur Lyons and featured such high-powered acting talents as Eric Roberts (brother of Julia, whose own promise of screen stardom has somehow eluded him), Beverly D'Angelo, Gerald McRaney and the wonderful Dan Hedaya.

Johnny played Donnie Fleischer, the spiky-haired, spoiled son of millionaire Hedaya, who is kidnapped, then murdered and dismembered (the second time Johnny died onscreen). The rest of the movie was a typical investigation into the crime. Unfortunately, the film never lived up to its potential and was quickly forgotten.

The film's executive producer, Joel Schumacher (also destined for greater success as the director of *St. Elmo's Fire, The Lost Boys* and *Batman Forever,* among others), remembered Johnny as "a very cool guy without putting much effort into being cool." Schumacher was also among the first to recognize the James Dean comparison. Without directly referring to a later Depp co-star, Robert Mitchum, he added, "He gave the impression that an acting career didn't matter to him all that much, yet he was always well prepared and approached each job with diligence."

But Johnny did care. Disappointed with the quality of roles he was playing and discouraged when he found himself out of work for a year, he followed the advice of Tracey Jacobs and enrolled in acting classes at the Loft Studio in Los Angeles.

Johnny plunged wholeheartedly into his workshops, determined to learn the intricacies of his newly chosen profession and give himself the opportunity to interact with other young, aspiring actors. An added bonus was that through these classes he met and began dating a budding young actress named Sherilyn Fenn (who would go on to movie and television success, most notably as Audrey Horne on David Lynch's quirky *Twin Peaks*). Within two months of their meeting, Johnny and Sherilyn were living together and planning to marry.

> Even with his new romantic involvement, Johnny stayed focused on his acting lessons, proving himself a much more conscientious student than what he'd shown during his formal schooling. Yet, while his confidence in his abilities continued to grow, he was still dismayed that movie offers were not forthcoming. At one particularly low point, Johnny even contemplated giving up acting

And then, in late 1985, he heard that Oscar-winning screen-writer Oliver Stone was preparing to direct a movie loosely based on his own Vietnam experience to be called *Platoon*. Johnny was one of many eager young actors to read for Stone, who he later recalled "scared the s*** out of me." Indeed, that was Stone's intention. He intended to put his players through a rough, tough regimen prior to lensing the film. He planned to march his 30 young actors through boot camp and 13 days of

combat training in the jungles of the Philippines under the command of real-life Vietnam veteran, Dale Dye.

Johnny and the other actors endured the life of military grunts, beginning with a 60-mile cross-country hike from Manilla into the heart of the jungle. Johnny slept in a foxhole that he and another actor dug by hand, went out on night patrol carrying full gear and even subsisted on cold army rations. Add to this the often-stifling humidity and high temperatures, it is little wonder that every one of the actors became ill at some point during the training.

Johnny later summed up the experience succinctly, "It was the toughest f***ing thing I ever had to do. Ever!"

But Stone knew that by putting his actors through the hellish survival training he and other Vietnam vets had endured, the experience would strengthen their characters and give them a greater believability in their acting.

Oliver Stone always intended *Platoon* to be an ensemble effort, with no one character shining above the others. Charlie Sheen, who played Private Chris Taylor, was the nominal star, but every member of the cast was important: from Tom Berenger's frighteningly intense, literally battle-scarred Sergeant Barnes and Willem Dafoe's sympathetic Sergeant Elias to supporting roles essayed by rising stars Forest Whitaker, Kevin Dillon and Francisco Quinn, lookalike son of the legendary Anthony.

In his review of the film, **New York Times** critic Vincent Canby noted, "The members of the supporting cast are no less fine than the principal players, and no less effective, often for being anonymous."

Johnny's role as the Vietnamese interpreter, Private Lerner, was one of the smaller parts, although the character had more screen time in the shooting script. Johnny was enthusiastic because the role provided an interesting and challenging opportunity, but he was disappointed when he saw the final cut. He appeared in only 11 scenes, and then only briefly. Johnny's most memorable moment comes when Lerner is shot in a jungle ambush and begs Private Taylor not to leave him. His bloody body is then transported aboard an evac helicopter, where he presumably succumbs to his wounds.

Despite the violent and depressing subject matter, *Platoon* was a surprise hit, scoring with critics and audiences alike. It garnered four Oscars, including Best Picture, earning a whopping $137,963,328 and becoming the Number Three top-grossing movie of the year, behind *Top Gun* and *Crocodile Dundee*. Oliver Stone's star was suddenly on the rise. Johnny, however, seemed almost lost in the shuffle.

His romance with Sheri-lyn Fenn had also run into problems. His long months in the Philippines coupled with the success she was beginning to achieve in her own career had caused the two to drift apart.

Despite his experiences on *Platoon*, Johnny looked forward to working again with Oliver Stone on a project

Johnny eagerly sought another movie role, but what he was most anticipating was his "big break." When it finally came, it was neither what he expected...or wanted.

called *Wonderland Now*, but the film (sort of a prelude to Stone's *The Doors*) ran into lengthy delays, and Johnny eventually dropped out.

He played for a while with a band called Rock City Angels, who signed a lucrative recording deal with David Geffen, but never released a second album.

Johnny eagerly sought another movie role, but what he was most anticipating was his "big break." When it finally came, it was neither what he expected…nor wanted.

chapter 3

Johnny's Jump Start

The project offered to Johnny was the lead role in a television series. Johnny had done one-shots on such shows as *Hotel* and the short-lived female "Dirty Harry" police drama *Lady Blue*, but he was not enthusiastic about committing to the weekly grind of a series.

The program was *Jump Street Chapel*, to be produced under the successful Stephen J. Cannell banner for Fox. Johnny was asked to read for the part of Officer Tom Hanson, one of a team of young undercover cops who pose as students to deal with high school crime issues. Johnny refused, even though no movie producers were breaking down his door with offers.

The show was re-christened *21 Jump Street,* and Jeff Yagher assumed the role intended for Johnny. However, within just three weeks of shooting, producer Steve Beers and creator Patrick Hasburgh knew that Yagher wasn't quite delivering and would have to be replaced. In desperation, they once again asked Johnny's agents to approach him. Johnny agreed to read the pilot script, and finally gave a tentative nod to do the series, *if* the show could eschew standard cop-show heroics and instead be used as a vehicle to impart positive messages to its young viewing audience.

Another reason Johnny accepted the role was that his agents explained to him that it was unlikely the series would last the season, given TV's "sausage factory" nature. But in the meantime, Johnny would collect a handsome pay packet of $45,000 per episode, build up a following and then have the freedom and resources to pursue his movie work.

Johnny finally gave a tentative nod to do the series, **if** the show could eschew standard cop-show heroics and instead be used as a vehicle to impart positive messages to its young viewing audience.

The contract that Johnny signed was the standard five-season agreement. Johnny thought the overall concept of the show was "fascist," but elements of the character intrigued him. Tom Hanson was a second-generation cop in his 20s who, despite having excelled at the police academy, looks too young to work effectively on the street. His superiors assign him to undercover high school duty where his liability is turned into an asset.

The show had some additional perks for Johnny, such as co-starring with a trio of talented young actors who played his fellow team members: Holly Robinson, Dustin Nguyen and Peter DeLuise (son of comic Dom and Johnny's closest friend on the series). From a professional standpoint, Johnny felt honored to be working with the respected character actor Frederic Forrest, who had delivered such outstanding performances in *Apocalypse Now* and *Hammett*. (Unfortunately, Forrest's character, Captain Fuller, only survived seven episodes of the first season before being killed by a drunk driver. His role was then filled by Steven Williams.)

The series was filmed in Vancouver, BC. Hoping to save his shaky relationship with Sherilyn Fenn, Johnny persuaded her to move north, with the added plum of a guest shot on one of the shows. He also invited his mother and stepfather to join him in Canada.

To Johnny's surprise, **21 Jump Street** became a hit. The previously little-known actor was suddenly a bona fide TV superstar, appealing primarily to a teenage audience, which was a position he was distinctly uncomfortable with. It bothered him that perhaps his talents were not so much recognized as his face, which was quickly plastered across every teen magazine in North America.

DEPP FAN FACT

21 Jump Street did have its genesis in reality, based on a controversial operation that had been in effect in Los Angeles since 1974.

What Johnny had hoped to avoid had become a reality. The series he believed would be canceled after its first season was renewed for a second with more in sight. And he was trapped into a five-year contract with little likelihood that the producers would release him from his commitment. Not when Johnny was receiving over 10,000 fan letters a month—more even than Michael J. Fox, then at the peak of his own television stardom with *Family Ties.*

To Johnny's credit, he never bad-mouthed the series. In interviews, he spoke favorably about the important issues the show covered, such as avoiding drugs and the importance of safe sex. He was grateful for the financial security the show provided, but he found little to embrace in the celebrity now thrust upon him. While he claimed that he didn't find fame "an ugly thing," everywhere he went he was mobbed by fans. Further, he felt a responsibility to personally answer the letters he received from troubled admirers who threatened to kill themselves unless he contacted them.

"This has to be the scariest part about this thing called 'celebrity,'" Johnny said. "Letters from girls threatening to jump off bridges if I don't get in touch with them. You want to think that it's all bulls***. But what if it's not? So I write them back and tell them just to hang in there. The thing is, I'm not altogether stable myself, so who am I to give advice? Besides, I'm just an actor, not a professional psychologist."

It didn't take long for the reluctant superstar to rebel against the pressures. To further aggravate the situation, the show's success became almost a straightjacket, precluding any film work Johnny might get unless it could be postponed until series hiatus. Johnny was in Canada and not yet a big enough mainstream marquee name to be granted such concessions.

Even though Johnny still would not slam the show outright in his interviews, he became more demanding on the set. He wanted more quality writing coupled with stronger, more meaningful story lines. Of course, his perfectionist behavior was interpreted by the tabloid press as "Fatheaded Johnny Depp Adopts Prima Donna Attitude on Set of Prime Time Super Hit."

Johnny would not quite agree with such an assessment, although he did admit that he became "a pain in the ass."

Did Johnny want off the show? Definitely. But he was sincere when he noted the deteriorating quality in some of the programs that he could liken to lukewarm police pablum.

> "My feeling is that the show needs to go deeper into certain issues, like racism and violence. I understand that there are strict boundaries in television, and there's only so much you can do, but the only way to change something is to fight it."

Coinciding with his professional disappointment was the inevitable end of his relationship with Sherilyn Fenn. Her role in the erotic *Two Moon Junction* looked to establish her as an actress with movie star potential, and she wanted to concentrate on her own opportunities rather than sitting in Canada watching her fiancé struggle with his career dissatisfactions.

All of Johnny's frustrations finally boiled over when he had an altercation with a security guard at a downtown Vancouver hotel. Johnny had lived at the hotel during his first season on *21 Jump Street* and was there one night to visit some friends. Johnny later claimed that the guard, who recognized him, accosted him and told him that unless he was a guest at the hotel he had no business roaming the halls. He said that the guard physically tried to remove him from the premises. Apparently, a scuffle ensued, ending with Johnny spitting in the guard's face. The whole ugly scene resulted in Johnny's being hauled away for an overnight stay in a Vancouver jail. Although charges were dropped, Johnny became prime tabloid fodder. He was labeled a "hell raiser," and for many years after would remain a favorite target of supermarket journalists.

Again Johnny offered **a succinct reply** to his critics: "I've got a bit of **a temper.**"

His comment would prove an understatement as Johnny would spend many years perpetuating his "hell raiser" image, providing the media with yards of juicy copy.

In a 2003 interview with *Entertainment Weekly*, Johnny confirmed the rumors that his dissatisfaction with the program had reached the point where he tried all sorts of antics to get himself booted off the show. These included appearing on the set with rubber bands wrapped around his tongue or reporting to work wearing a feathered turban or a George Washington wig along with hip-hugging bell-bottoms with the American flag stitched across the crotch.

Then, during the third season of *21 Jump Street*, the producers added a "safety valve" to the series by introducing the character of Booker, played by Richard Grieco, who was also equipped with the dark, brooding looks and intensity of Johnny Depp.

"It was a frustrating time. I didn't feel I was doing anybody any good on there. Not the people who watch the show. Certainly not myself."

Ironically, the character of Booker proved so popular that he was given his own series, entitled *Booker*. While Johnny's appearances were shortened considerably when Booker was on *21 Jump Street*, with the character now featured on his own program, the producers again pleaded with Johnny to commit to more screen time to save the now-sinking series.

Yet Johnny could not muster the enthusiasm to go on with the show, and his sparse appearances continued. Despite the talents of his co-stars, their contribution did not possess the glue required to hold the show together. It was clear by the ratings that Johnny *was 21 Jump Street*. The show's producers finally agreed to release him from the time remaining on his contract, and on July 16, 1990, audiences watched Johnny play his final scene as Officer Tom Hanson.

As Johnny later explained, "It was a frustrating time. I didn't feel I was doing anybody any good on there. Not the people who watch the show. Certainly not myself."

After five years of "creative bondage" Johnny Depp was finally free. He had regained his artistic independence. Now all he had to do was find a job.

chapter 4

treading into unknown
"Waters"

The TV series *21 Jump Street* provided Johnny with a solid base from which he could either sink or swim. If he chose to capitalize on his television success, he could grab the multitude of offers that would further exploit his popular image and, conceivably, enjoy a few years garnering TV or B-movie credits before being consigned to oblivion. Or he could assign this substantial but ultimately suffocating credit to the back page of his resume and move forward in an entirely different professional direction.

Johnny probably never debated his decision for a moment. He quickly turned down *any* role that even remotely resembled Tom Hanson. He had enough faith in his talents and versatility to amicably, yet completely, divorce himself from his TV alter ego.

Perhaps Hollywood's heavy-hitters weren't inundating Johnny with creative script material, but one Baltimore-based filmmaker conceived a role that might forever separate Johnny Depp the actor from that stifling, yet overwhelming, television image.

The word that best describes John Waters' movie achievements is "tasteless." Such is his reputation for putrid celluloid that a recent biography of the director is simply titled *Filthy*. It is hard to imagine any serious artist appreciating his career being encapsulated under such a heading, but Waters is less offended by the term than most audiences who endure his cinematic excesses.

He became (and remains) a cult figure thanks to endless midnight showings of his notorious 1972 "masterpiece" *Pink Flamingos*, starring that obese and obscene transvestite

Divine. While his films may have proved satisfying to his artistic sensibilities, their financial compensations were minimal, and Waters finally decided to compromise his creative standards—if barely—to keep from starving.

He first allowed himself entry into mainstream cinema with *Hairspray* (1988), Waters' bizarre, if affectionate, tribute to the TV dance crazes of the early Sixties. Waters further cast his film with such diverse and eccentric talent as Divine, Sonny Bono, Deborah Harry, Ricki Lake, Jerry Stiller and Pia Zadora.

The film set no fires at the box office, so Waters plunged a little deeper into traditional moviemaking with his next feature, *Cry-Baby*. The concept had a commercial attraction sufficient to secure a distribution deal from Universal Studios.

Waters fashioned his screenplay on the Romeo and Juliet theme, updated to 1954 and set it in his own hometown of Baltimore. The story is a simple fable of the love affair between leather-jacketed, tough Wade Walker and rich girl Allison Vernon-Williams. Of course, Waters adds his own special blend of peculiarities to the outwardly simplistic story line, notably Wade's profound sensitivity (hence the film's title).

Waters again had fun with his individualized casting, selecting "jailbait" porn star Traci Lords, the infamous heiress-turned-terrorist Patty Hearst and Johnny Depp's old nemesis Iggy Pop for featured roles. (Divine was also included on the cast list, but succumbed to a heart attack before the start of production.)

Waters' biggest problem was finding his lead player. He knew *what* he needed—a dreamy, heartthrob hunk—only he didn't know where to find him. In desperation, he scoured the teen magazines to see who was currently "hot." What he discovered was the pouty face of Johnny Depp on the cover of virtually every

Johnny had enough faith in his talents and versatility to amicably, yet completely, divorce himself from his TV alter ego.

Cry-Baby (1990)

publication. Waters decided to surrender to possible serendipity, and he sent Johnny a copy of the *Cry-Baby* screenplay.

Johnny read the script and immediately set up a meeting with Waters. Despite the director's openly homosexual leanings and Johnny's complete heterosexuality, the two shared a somewhat warped creative bond that superseded personal intimate preferences and resulted in a unique professional collaboration.

> **Waters later recalled, "Johnny was sick and tired of being hyped as a teen idol, and I suggested that the best way to get rid of an image was to make a parody of it."**

While John Waters' previous basement-budget productions might not have provided the proper vehicle for Johnny to reinvent himself, *Cry-Baby* had a budget of $8 million. Johnny's own commercial value was made apparent by the fact that a mere six years earlier he had earned $7200 for *A Nightmare on Elm Street*. For *Cry-Baby*, only his fifth movie, he was reportedly paid $1 million, heady progress for a high school dropout who had foreseen only a bleak or, if lucky, blue-collar future for himself. Yet, Johnny remained modest and unaffected by his sudden accumulation of wealth and fame.

His boyhood friend Sal Jenco once remarked during the early days of Johnny's success, "There's just no bulls*** with him. He's a completely straight guy who's adjusted to his celebrity the same way he would have taken a minimum wage job pumping gas."

Cry-Baby created no tidal waves at the domestic box office but became a cult favorite in the overseas market. Johnny was happy with his European and Australian recognition, which not only erased his television signature role but also started him on the road to full-fledged movie stardom.

Johnny's next movie role proved even more eccentric than his playing in *Cry-Baby*, yet it was the part that would not only guarantee his future stardom, but also highlight Johnny Depp as the screen's most individual performer.

The concept of *Edward Scissorhands* originated in the mind of Tim Burton, a man who might best be described as Steven Spielberg without restraint. Both share personal and professional similarities, including a love of horror/monster movies that molded their individual creative consciousness. They admit to digesting each new issue of Forrest J. Ackerman's seminal monster magazine *Famous Monsters of Filmland* as if it were a fresh bowl of Halloween candy. Beyond the genre aesthetics, both shared a fascination with the mechanics of moviemaking, the tactile thrill of examining developed color celluloid, the result of their own basement or backyard 8mm movie masterpieces—crude efforts that nonetheless were testaments to imaginative ingenuity later showcased in multi-milliondollar studio productions.

Tim Burton is a true individual—a strange-looking, self-professed "outsider" who experienced the pain of childhood rejection among his peers. One way he dealt with his loneliness was through his art. After high school, he attended the California Institute of the Arts, enrolling in the school's animation department. Burton's unique talents were instantly recognized, and he was accepted into the Disney program, where he was assigned work on *The Fox and the Hound*. However, he didn't find such work creatively satisfying. His passion was in designing bizarre imagery.

So, during his spare time he created the animated short *Vincent*, a semi-biographical tribute to Burton's movie idol, Vincent Price. The success of the short led to other film work, including *Frankenweenie* and his first all-out commercial hit *Pee-wee's Big Adventure*. But where Burton really established his reputation as a filmmaker of dark, personal vision was with *Beetlejuice* and *Batman*, starring an unlikely Michael

Johnny was not Burton's first choice for the title role. Burton went for big box office and approached superstar Tom Cruise...

42

Keaton as the caped vigilante and the perfectly cast Jack Nicholson as the psychotic Joker.

Each of these films, however, stood as a prelude to Burton's most intimate movie: a contemporary fable dealing with the ultimate misfit who tried to fit into the stifling complacency of middle-class suburbia. Burton called his film *Edward Scissorhands*.

Johnny was not Burton's first choice for the title role. Burton went for big box office and approached superstar Tom Cruise, who initially expressed interest in portraying the Frankenstein-like humanoid, but then opted out because he felt the necessary application of Edward's facial scars would be distracting. Michael Jackson and even Tom Hanks were then considered before a copy of the script was submitted to Johnny's agent.

Johnny read the script and was "blown away" by both the character and Tim Burton's imaginative story. Burton agreed to a meeting, but was not particularly enthusiastic about casting Johnny in the role because he'd really only thought of the actor as a teen idol without much substance.

Johnny, on the other hand, considered *Edward Scissorhands* a once-in-a-lifetime part. Even though he could well understand Burton's reserve in hiring him, he did everything he could to convince Burton that he *was* the right person for the role. After their meeting, Burton spent a few hours watching Johnny's rough edit work in *Cry-Baby*, then called Johnny to say, "You are Edward Scissorhands."

One of the character points that most intrigued Johnny was Edward's lack of dialogue. This was almost unheard of in modern-day cinema. Johnny's challenge would be to convey to the audience Edward's myriad yet stilted emotions through Chaplinesque pantomime.

Edward Scissorhands (1990)

Edward Scissorhands is a magical film, an enchanting if ultimately haunting fairy tale, surreal yet identifiable in its setting: a landscape of pastel-colored tract housing, each home a virtual replica of its neighbor. Yet existing just beyond this tranquil, if monotonous, community stands the Gothic castle of the inventor, played by Vincent Price who, in his loneliness, creates Edward as his companion. Sadly, the old inventor dies of a heart attack before he can graft real hands onto his creation, leaving Edward equipped with the garden-clipper appendages the old man had previously attached to his arms. A bewildered Edward is soon discovered by an Avon lady (Dianne Wiest), who takes pity on the strange fellow and naïvely takes him home, where he becomes an object of curiosity and fascination among her neighbors. The story explores such themes as the plight of one unable to conform to middle-class hypocrisy, the cruelty of teenage cliques and the angst of adolescent romance. Each of these subplots is given sensitive treatment with Tim Burton's direction and Johnny's brilliant playing.

Johnny, along with Burton, knew the hurt of not fitting in and was able to parlay those feelings into a masterful rendering of a creature that never asked to be born. Abandoned by his creator (father), Edward strives to be accepted into an environment he does not understand. He returns compassion with compassion, but when his gentle nature is threatened, he strikes back with an aggression he likewise does not fully comprehend. Johnny proves himself an actor of ability by wordlessly conveying these emotions through skillful body gestures and taut yet effective facial expressions, most notably with the wonderment in his eyes.

Johnny rejected Burton's original idea to have his razor fingers manipulated by off-stage puppeteers. He insisted on operating the lethal-looking but harmless blades himself.

According to Burton, Johnny felt he could not become the character unless he personally understood the frustrations Edward would encounter dealing with his "handicap," and so he spent long hours correctly choreographing the intricate maneuverings of his "scissorhands" until he mastered a ballet-like precision with his prostheses.

Johnny's efforts paid off. *Edward Scissorhands* was released on December 7, 1990, and went on to gross over $54 million in domestic video rentals. His own performance was critically applauded, and he received a Golden Globe nomination for Best Actor in a Motion Picture: Comedy/Musical.

"The character was the **closest to me**," Johnny admitted. "He was a **little boy in the brain**. A really small child."

The film began a profitable working relationship between Johnny and a director who initially hadn't wanted him for the part. But Tim Burton later said, "I'm glad Johnny played Edward. I can't think of anyone else who would have done it quite as well."

Johnny explained the successful working relationship between Burton and himself, "We both grew up in suburbia. And we both had a fascination with horror movies and horror characters from a young age. I can remember sitting in the first grade drawing pictures of Frankenstein and Dracula. Later, when I was a little older, I wanted to be Barnabas Collins [the well-known soap opera vampire from Dark Shadows]."

Johnny also enjoyed having the opportunity to both work with and befriend Vincent Price in the twilight years of the legendary actor's life. As with most of Johnny's veteran co-stars, Price was high in his praise of Johnny's talents: "Depp is as skilled and adept an actor as any I've worked with in my career."

Edward Scissorhands co-starred 27-year-old Johnny with 18-year-old Winona Ryder. The two had been dating prior to their work on the film, and it was Johnny who recommended Winona for the role of Dianne Wiest's daughter, Kim, a suggestion to which Burton was agreeable since he had already recognized her talents in *Beetlejuice*.

Johnny's relationship with Winona was the most serious involvement he had yet enjoyed. The feelings the two shared for each other were so genuine, they transcend the playing of their *Scissorhands* scenes. He was so sure that their love would be lasting that he had "Winona Forever" tattooed on his arm. (He also has his mother's name Betty Sue tattooed across his left bicep.)

Of course, their romance provided tabloid journalists with mountains of copy, and both tried to maintain a low profile, which proved a difficult if not impossible task with the success of Tim Burton's movie transforming Johnny Depp and Winona Ryder into overnight movie superstars.

chapter 5

Fear and Celebrity in Los Angeles

Movie stardom is an exalted position that every hungry actor aspires to. The perks are many and include money, parties, premieres, travel, adulation and VIP treatment at all the best hotels and restaurants. This kind of celebrity also opens doors for hobnobbing with the rich and powerful. The car valet of yesterday may tomorrow appear as a guest on *Oprah* or rub shoulders with Donald Trump.

Johnny, however, was determined not to fall into what he perceived to be the "trap of celebrity." He'd experienced his tough younger years and also endured the peaks and valleys of the acting profession. Now that he had once again achieved status in the industry, he wanted to keep his fame in perspective.

Perhaps Johnny was more conscious of the downside of the business. With the release of *Edward Scissorhands*, he began attracting his share of weirdo admirers—some of whom had related too closely to Johnny's character because they, too, had experienced the pain of rejection and alienation. Rather than seeking counseling for their problems, these individuals, whose grasp on reality was tenuous at best, sought out Johnny instead.

Johnny sorted through the death threats he received and letters in which more seriously disturbed persons believed that *they* were the real Johnny Depp and that he was the imposter.

"Sometimes it's unreal and frightening out there," Johnny said.

And Johnny couldn't ignore the reality of the "stalker syndrome"—a perverse status symbol that indicated he had made it. Crazies aside, however,

> The car valet of yesterday may tomorrow appear as a guest on *Oprah* or rub shoulders with Donald Trump.

what mattered most to Johnny was that he was now regarded as an actor of range and depth.

Not that such acknowledged success decreased his professional idiosyncrasies. It was as if with sudden stardom now upon him, Johnny went out of his way to avoid big-budget commercial productions. He turned down the lead role in *Speed*, which propelled Keanu Reeves into screen stardom.

Johnny then further rejected two roles he didn't feel suited for— *Legends of the Fall* and *Interview with the Vampire*—both of which were inherited by *Dallas* alumnus, Brad Pitt, likewise making him a box office draw. Instead, Johnny chose to repay a favor to Wes Craven (who had given Johnny his first break) and Rachel Talalay (the producer on *Cry-Baby*) by appearing in a cameo role in the latest installment of the *Elm Street* saga: *Freddy's Dead: The Final Nightmare*.

> Johnny, recognizable but billed as "Oprah Noodlemantra," appears in a mock public service announcement where, in a take-off on a popular ad campaign of the time, he likens an egg frying in a pan to "your brain on drugs."

The next film on Johnny's agenda was again one where audience acceptance was negligible. What appealed to Johnny was the opportunity to work with filmmaker Emir Kusturica. The Yugoslavian-born director had already received critical acclaim for his award-winning productions *Time of the Gypsies, Underground* and *When Father Was Away on Business.* Johnny was particularly eager to sign up for Kusturica's *Arizona Dream* because he considered *Time of the Gypsies* "one of the most amazing films I'd ever seen."

Arizona Dream was shot on location in Alaska, Arizona and New York and was budgeted at $17 million. The picture was a dream project for Kusturica, further enhanced by a strong supporting cast, including Jerry Lewis, Faye Dunaway and the underrated Lili Taylor. But Kusturica's "dream" quickly evolved into a nightmare. The shooting proved difficult, and at one point, the director suffered a nervous collapse. When the film's producers threatened to replace Kusturica, the cast, championed by Johnny, threatened to walk off the picture. Kusturica recovered to complete the movie, which was awarded a special Jury Prize at the Berlin Festival in 1993. The following year, the movie proved a smash hit in Paris (due, in no small part, to Jerry Lewis' enormous popularity with French audiences). Despite this, *Arizona Dream*, even after radical editing, was deemed too "quirky" for American taste, and the film's distributor Warner Brothers released it directly to video.

Johnny was disappointed at the fate of a movie for which he'd had such enthusiasm. He was also upset for Kusturica after all the difficulties the director had undergone to make the film. But both men's spirits were uplifted when they began discussing plans to make another movie together, an intriguing updated retelling of Dostoevsky's *Crime and Punishment.* Yet, despite having a script and financial

Johnny was particularly eager to sign up for Kusturica's **Arizona Dream** because he considered **Time of the Gypsies** "one of the most amazing films I'd ever seen."

Benny & Joon (1993)

negotiations completed, the Italian funding suddenly disappeared, and the project fell through.

Johnny's attraction to quirky movie projects continued with *Benny & Joon*. The film was conceived as a '90s-style screwball comedy/romance that centers on a blue-collar worker named Benny who sacrifices his own happiness to care for his emotionally and mentally disturbed sister, Joon. Johnny plays Sam, an oddball circus acrobat who has the uncanny ability to communicate with the girl, thus earning Benny's ire.

As with *Arizona Dream*, the production was troubled. Casting was the primary problem. First, Tom Hanks was announced as Benny with Julia Roberts as Joon, then real-life marrieds Tim Robbins and Susan Sarandon. Finally, Woody Harrelson and Laura Dern came onboard, only to jump ship when Dern received an Oscar nomination for *Rambling Rose*, and Harrelson was offered the role of the husband opposite Demi Moore and Robert Redford in *Indecent Proposal*.

Finally, lesser lights Aidan Quinn, a couple of years away from ***Legends of the Fall***, and Mary Stuart Masterson, who'd delivered a memorable performance in ***Fried Green Tomatoes***, signed for the title roles.

It seemed that only Johnny remained enthusiastic about the film. He was happy to work with Canadian-born director Jeremiah Chechik, whose previous movie credit was the Chevy Chase hit *National Lampoon's Christmas Vacation*. Chechik allowed Johnny freedom to experiment with his character's physical eccentricities. Of course, Johnny's gift for pantomime had already been displayed in *Edward Scissorhands*, but in that film he had played an exaggerated artificial creation. As Sam, he was a flesh-and-blood human being who had to perfect more subtly many of the physical skills required. He admitted spending hours watching silent movies, absorbing the artistry of

Charlie Chaplin, Buster Keaton and Harold Lloyd. The rest of his training came from a professional mime.

> **When the film was released in 1993, Johnny's effective rendering of pratfalls and pathos so impressed British director Sir Richard Attenborough that he offered Johnny the role of Charlie Chaplin in his upcoming film biography of that comedian. Johnny was flattered, but he bowed out, saying that it was an overwhelming task. Robert Downey Jr. replaced him, and his efforts earned the talented actor an Academy Award nomination.**

Benny & Joon received mostly positive reviews, with Johnny's performance singled out for praise. Unfortunately, the film just did not catch on with audiences.

Johnny was disappointed by the movie's poor box office. He'd given a performance of which he was especially proud. He vented some of his anger on the Hollywood powers-that-be. "People don't just want to see a parade of nudity and violence. I think movie executives have badly underestimated the movie-going public."

Concerning his role in the movie and his apparent preference for playing oddballs, Johnny remarked, "I guess you could say that freaks are my heroes."

Even with two back-to-back box office failures, Johnny remained in demand. Sadly, perhaps inevitably, Johnny's romantic life again took a nosedive. In June 1993, Johnny and Winona Ryder officially called off their engagement. Much of the blame

"People don't just want to see a parade of nudity and violence. I think movie executives have badly underestimated the movie-going public."

could be placed on the press. Although their romance was saleable copy, so were the hints of infidelity and battles fueled by Johnny's famous temper. Gossip columnists now linked Winona to her co-stars, Gary Oldman (Bram Stoker's *Dracula*) and Daniel Day-Lewis (*The Age of Innocence*). With rumors and accusations compounding increasing professional demands, the two parted.

> Neither wanted to discuss their breakup publicly, although Winona eventually issued a cryptic statement: "It was a really good thing that it ended. I don't know how much the media had to do with it because we really had drifted apart a long time before the press found out that it had ended. I think [Johnny's] great, and I have nothing but kind things to say about him, but it was just over."

When pressed, Johnny responded philosophically, saying that their parting followed a "natural progression," and that he was happy they were still friends.

In truth, Johnny was heartbroken. He had his "Winona Forever" tattoo surgically altered to read "Wino Forever," and to a great degree that was the path he now followed. According to a friend, Johnny just could not accept the permanence of their breakup, and to cope with his depression he began drinking and smoking heavily, eating badly and in general ignoring his health completely.

> In truth, Johnny was heartbroken. He had his "Winona Forever" tattoo surgically altered to read "Wino Forever," and to a great degree that was the path he now followed.

Fortunately, he had his movie work to focus on—although the period preceding and during the making of *What's Eating Gilbert Grape* likely represents the lowest, if not the darkest time in Johnny Depp's life.

In August 1993, Johnny and partner Chuck E. Weiss purchased a Sunset Boulevard nightclub for a reported $350,000. They named the club the Viper Room and intended to use it as a place where Johnny and his pals could hang out and listen to a selection of eclectic musical preferences. The club would also provide a venue for upcoming musicians to try out their material.

Johnny entered the venture hoping to create an appreciation for musical nostalgia. But the club was already famous for nostalgia of a different sort. Back in the 1930s, the club was called The Central and was owned by the notorious gangster Charles "Lucky" Luciano and frequented by his pal Benjamin "Bugsy" Siegel, then making criminal inroads into Hollywood society. Perhaps Johnny knew of the club's checkered past because he chose to decorate its interior in the style of a 1920s speakeasy, complete with cigarette girls.

The Viper Room soon became a popular watering hole for "young Hollywood," including a 23-year-old actor who had already made his mark in the movie business. River Phoenix had starred in some of Hollywood's most popular films, including *Stand by Me* and *Indiana Jones and the Temple of Doom*. He was a talented, versatile actor who had just signed to play the writer opposite Tom Cruise and Brad Pitt in the long-antici- pated film version of Anne Rice's bestseller *Interview With the Vampire* (a movie that Johnny had turned down).

He also enjoyed being recognized as a positive role model to his young fans, an advocate of healthy living with his vegan diet and most especially avoidance of alcohol and drugs. Sadly, River Phoenix's death within just two hours of entering the Viper Room proved him a total contradiction.

Young River had a lot to celebrate that night. He was particularly looking forward to taking to the stage to perform some of his own musical compositions. Apparently, River had begun "partying" much earlier that evening. By the time he arrived at the club with his brother, sister and girlfriend, he was noticeably intoxicated.

At some point, River disappeared into the men's room where he became violently ill after someone gave him some Peruvian Brown. To calm him down, someone then offered him Valium. Shortly after 1:00 AM, he staggered from the club, where he collapsed on the pavement and went into convulsions. At approximately 1:45 AM, River Phoenix was dead.

Johnny was devastated by the tragedy. He was in the club that night and was playing onstage with some musician friends about the time River overdosed. Although he and River were not close friends, he felt the loss deeply.

Once again, the tabloids had a "sensational" Depp story to sell their readers. Johnny was forced to go public to explain that his club was not a notorious drug den, that what happened to River Phoenix was an unfortunate yet isolated occurrence.

Sunset Boulevard is not the street of dreams once portrayed in Hollywood history. Today, vagrants, panhandlers and the homeless populate it. Some are screen hopefuls living on the charity of nickels and dimes, hoping to sustain themselves long enough until their lucky break. Others are just pathetic castoffs of society. But whatever their circumstances, Johnny sympathizes with them, just as he will never forget the terrible events of October 31, 1993. He often walks that stretch of concrete

Sunset Boulevard is not the street of dreams once portrayed in Hollywood history. Today, vagrants, panhandlers and the homeless populate it.

DEPP FAN FACT

Christian Slater replaced River Phoenix, but *Interview with a Vampire* is dedicated to him.

outside his club during the pre-dawn hours, handing out money to those who have no food or no place to go.

Perhaps the unnecessary loss of such a promising talent prompted Johnny to take a brotherly interest in his young *What's Eating Gilbert Grape* co-star, Leonardo DiCaprio. Leonardo was first noticed as a teenage heartthrob on the popular sitcom *Growing Pains*, supplanting the popularity of the show's original pin-up boy, Kirk Cameron. Cameron willingly disassociated himself from his teen magazine image once he developed strong religious convictions, which he maintains today.

Leonardo was brought in to boost sagging ratings during the series' 1991–92 season, and his role as the homeless Luke Browser instantly caught the attention of young audiences. Despite voluminous magazine coverage, Leonardo remained grounded, his level-headedness earning the respect of co-stars Alan Thicke and Joanna Kerns.

While still maintaining his sexy teen image, Leonardo was soon recognized for his abilities as an actor. He appeared in three films, including *This Boy's Life*, opposite Robert De Niro. *What's Eating Gilbert Grape*, however, provided Leonardo with his most challenging

> Perhaps the unnecessary loss of such a promising talent prompted Johnny to take a brotherly interest in his young ***What's Eating Gilbert Grape*** co-star, Leonardo DiCaprio.

role yet. He played Arnie, the mentally impaired brother of Gilbert (Johnny Depp), who assumes the "father figure" role in the household after the suicide of their real dad. Besides looking after Arnie and his two sisters, Gilbert has the added responsibility of caring for his 600-pound mother, whose obesity has prevented her for years from leaving the house. Gilbert feels equally stifled by his work as a grocery store clerk and finds that even this mundane employment is threatened by the opening of a major supermarket just outside town. Gilbert's whole life changes when he meets a young woman named Becky (Juliette Lewis), who is forced to spend a few days in Endora, Texas, when her motor home breaks down.

Johnny received good reviews for a role in which he affected unflattering physical alterations to enhance his characterization, including having his teeth bonded and chipped and dyeing his lengthy hair a rather ghastly shade of red. But it was Leonardo DiCaprio who emerged as the star of the show. Having learned about intense preparation from his former co-star Robert De Niro, Leonardo immersed himself in research. He met with mentally challenged individuals, studying their mannerisms and speech patterns so that he could deliver an accurate, honest depiction of the character. But he was overwhelmed by the many variables attributed to the challenged, so Leonardo finally limited his focus and drew his inspiration for the role from one autistic boy.

Leonardo also gave credit for his Oscar-nominated performance to Johnny, saying that he could never have been quite so convincing in the part if not for the real-life bonding between the two. Johnny had established an immediate rapport with the younger actor and enjoyed playing a series of good-natured practical jokes on him, which Leonardo gamely went along with. One of their favorites was when Johnny would present Leonardo with a collection of foul-smelling items, ranging from rotten eggs to a decayed honeycomb

> Leonardo also gave credit for his Oscar-nominated performance to Johnny, saying that he could never have been quite so convincing in the part if not for the real-life bonding between the two.

What's Eating Gilbert Grape (1993)

and then hoot with laughter when Leonardo reacted with animated expressions to their stench. The game proved profitable to Leonardo, as he won about $500 accepting Johnny's dares.

Leonardo later described the real Johnny Depp as "extremely nice and cool. But at the same time, he's hard to figure out."

Leonardo's observation is a true assessment of Johnny's often-enigmatic personality. But Johnny was deeply troubled during the production because he was still mourning his breakup with Winona and the tragic loss of River Phoenix. The memories affect him so much that to this day he has refused to watch the film. However, he confessed that playing the role of Gilbert Grape had special meaning to him.

> "There are incidents in my life that directly parallel things that happen to Gilbert. I understand that feeling of suffocating from being stuck in a place, either geographical or emotional. I can understand the rage of just wanting to escape from everything and everybody you know and just make a new life."

Perhaps that is another reason Johnny has avoided seeing the movie. Because so much of his true self was revealed on camera, and the part just hits too close to home.

What's Eating Gilbert Grape opened Christmas Day, 1993. Its total domestic earnings amounted to a disappointing $9,170,214,

But Johnny was deeply troubled during the production because he was still mourning his breakup with Winona and the tragic loss of River Phoenix.

Johnny's third lowest box office showing next to *Cry-Baby* ($7,735,790) and *Arizona Dream* ($106,658). Johnny's ongoing depression over personal matters was hardly alleviated by enduring yet another commercial flop. He continued with his self-destructive lifestyle.

It is highly possible that Johnny Depp might have become another "dead before their time" celebrity statistic had he not experienced a frightening wake-up call. He later recalled that he was sitting with some friends when he suddenly experienced what he thought was a severe "anxiety attack." His heart was racing, and when it wouldn't slow down he realized that whatever he was experiencing was more than anxiety. He had his friends drive him to the hospital, where he was administered a shot that brought him back to earth. Having survived this truly scary ordeal, Johnny decided to work at getting his body back into shape.

chapter 6

Wood And
Moss

johnny's career disappointments were, at least temporarily, assuaged with his next movie—another collaboration with Tim Burton, director of *Edward Scissorhands*, his most financially successfully movie so far. This film would highlight another "Edward," although Ed D. Wood Jr. was not a screenwriter's fiction, but a real person, a character with those requisite eccentric traits that Johnny seemed to embrace creatively.

Who would think that any movie simply titled *Ed Wood* would have any marquee value?

Answer: The vast multitude of bad film aficionados worldwide.

Ed Wood is a film that probably never would have been made if not for a book called *The Golden Turkey Awards* co-authored by brothers Harry and Michael Medved. This book, a lighthearted but somewhat stinging compendium of Hollywood's worst cinematic achievements, awards the late Ed Wood the dubious "honor" of "Worst Director of All Time," and his movie *Plan Nine from Outer Space* as "Worst Movie of All Time."

Suddenly, the rediscovery of Wood's forgotten film work initiated an Ed Wood cult. Video companies such as Canada's Admit One were building an industry by obtaining the rights to, then releasing to tape, the worst movies ever made. These titles, including *Attack of the 50-Foot Woman, The Brain That Wouldn't Die* and the unforgettable *They Saved Hitler's Brain* were preceded to the video market by the output of Ed Wood.

The legacy of Ed Wood was further showcased or, more

Ed Wood (1994)

precisely, ridiculed by Paramount Pictures bad film retrospective *It Came from Hollywood.*

The idea for a biopic on Ed Wood originated with two USC film school graduates, Scott Alexander and Larry Karaszewski, who had already cut their teeth as industry screenwriters with *Problem Child.* They produced a 147-page screenplay for *Ed Wood,* which they pitched to Tim Burton. Burton, who had just dropped out of *Mary Reilly,* another retelling of the Dr. Jekyll and Mr. Hyde story, was enthusiastic about the script and agreed to direct it.

Burton's first decision was to film the movie in black and white, a concept that hardly met with unanimous approval by the executives at Columbia, under whose production banner the picture was to be made. Burton then approached Disney, for whom he'd made the successful *A Nightmare Before Christmas,* and they agreed to bankroll and distribute the movie.

Burton immediately **chose Johnny** to play the **title role**, and after a brief coffeehouse meeting between the two, **Johnny committed to the project.**

Ed Wood covered only the director's early to mid-point career, from his association with producer George Weiss and the making of *Glen or Glenda,* through his struggles to obtain financing for *Bride of the Monster* and finally to the wholly fictionalized "gala" premiere of *Plan Nine from Outer Space.*

Central to the plot was the friendship between a struggling young movie director and an aging, forgotten horror star. Ed Wood's enormous admiration for Bela Lugosi mirrored Tim Burton's own great personal and professional respect for Vincent Price. Although Price was not quite the neglected horror icon Lugosi had become, Burton saw the faded star and witnessed the physical decline of a man his childhood perceptions had considered "bigger than life."

Having noted the close comradeship Johnny and Leonardo DiCaprio had enjoyed on *Gilbert Grape*, Burton knew it was imperative that he match Johnny with an actor who could convey the dramatic power of Bela Lugosi, while also displaying a genuine personal affection for his young worshipper.

Burton scored an excellent choice in Martin Landau, who absorbed himself so completely in his role that he won a Best Supporting Actor Academy Award. Landau's transformation into the latter-day screen bogeyman is remarkable. Aided by makeup Oscar-winner Rick Baker who rendered Landau's familiar visage almost unrecognizable, Landau mastered the complexities of Lugosi's personality so well that many commented that the late actor himself must have channeled his spirit into Landau.

More importantly, despite some reported early wariness between Johnny and Landau, the two actors quickly discovered a respect for each other's professionalism, and their friendship spilled over into their on-camera relationship. Landau was another actor who likened Johnny to James Dean, whom Landau had known well back during their early days in New York. Landau went so far as to call Johnny "Jimmy's only credible heir."

While Martin Landau certainly provided *Ed Wood* with the movie's showcase role, Burton carefully rounded out his cast with such capable talent as Sarah Jessica Parker (Dolores Fuller), Patricia Arquette (Kathy Wood), Lisa Marie (Vampira), Jeffrey Jones (Criswell), Bill Murray (Bunny Breckenridge), among others who played characters that were an integral part of Ed Wood's circle.

Where *Ed Wood* fails on an aesthetic level is that it is not an accurate portrayal of the director's life and struggles. Dolores Fuller is portrayed as an initially supportive, but ultimately frustrated, partner of Ed's dreams. In truth, Miss Fuller helped keep Ed Wood financially

Landau was another actor who likened Johnny to James Dean, whom Landau had known well back during their early days in New York. Landau went so far as to call Johnny "Jimmy's only credible heir."

afloat with her own well-paying work, and left him only when his drinking got out of hand.

Johnny's portrayal of Eddie has its own factual fallacies, particularly with Johnny's decision to express the character's buoyant enthusiasm by displaying a perpetual grin. Johnny concurred. He later remarked that after making the movie "I couldn't shake that grin for months."

> The most complex aspect of playing Ed Wood was his well-publicized passion for wearing women's clothing, particularly panties and angora sweaters. Ed was certainly not gay, to which Miss Fuller would instantly attest; rather he enjoyed the closeness he felt about the feminine body by donning their clothing.

Johnny was never averse to assuming physical transformations not conducive to his "Hollywood" image if he felt it suited the character he was playing. With Ed Wood, he really had little choice, since Eddie was a real person. Johnny accepted the challenge with no trepidation.

Overall, the part provided Johnny with a welcome change from all the emotionally confused and troubled individuals he'd been playing. He had high expectations for this film and admitted that it was the first time he was actually excited about seeing one of his performances.

"This movie gave me a really good departure from any of the other s*** that I've done," he remarked.

And Johnny's work was rewarded with a Golden Globe nomination, which he lost to Hugh Grant for his role in *Four Weddings and a Funeral*.

Ed Wood was a labor of love for all concerned. Perhaps more importantly, the movie is respectful of an ambitious and (within

DEPP FAN FACT

Ed Wood was another Johnny Depp movie that fared better in Europe, where it received a premiere screening at the Cannes Film Festival.

his limits) dedicated man never accepted by Hollywood mainstream. That is why it is all the more unfortunate that the Halloween 1994 release brought in dismal domestic revenues of only $5,828,466.

> Even if *Ed Wood* was Tim Burton's first film to flounder, Johnny still embraced the creative joy the movie had provided. But what brought him personal happiness was his new romantic relationship with British supermodel Kate Moss.

Kate and Johnny shared professional similarities. She had never aspired to a modeling career. She was actually discovered when, at the age of 14, Sarah Doukas of Britain's Storm Agency spotted her at New York's Kennedy Airport. Kate began modeling during summer vacations and, during the early 1990s, established an international reputation for her waif-like look. In 1993, she signed a $1 million contract with Calvin Klein.

Johnny first met Kate Moss at Café Tabac in New York City. Kate later admitted that while she did not feel a "love-at-first-sight" attraction to Johnny, she did believe that they would be together. Which was exactly the case, as the couple was soon photographed at several social and charitable functions.

Despite an 11-year age difference between the two, Kate possessed a maturity that bridged the gap. She was only 21, and her modeling fame was already eclipsing the movie stardom of her boyfriend.

Johnny was deeply in love with Kate, and he responded graciously to most press queries regarding their relationship. The only time he took offense was when asked about her super-slim figure, which some suggested might encourage bulimia or anorexia among young girls.

Johnny countered with: "Kate eats like a champ. She's being criticized because her metabolism is more active than most people's."

Although the couple appeared deliriously happy, rumors were spreading among friends and past acquaintances that there was already "trouble in paradise." A former girlfriend stepped forward to say that she was concerned about Johnny's frequent temper flare-ups. Although Johnny insisted he had given up his heavy drinking when he met Kate, he was still dealing with inner turmoil and insecurities that could, on occasion, explode to the surface.

What Johnny wanted in his life was the security of a wife and family. Yet he wondered if he could ever truly realize such an ideal. He'd certainly acquired the financial means by which to raise a family in comfort. But he was also afraid that because he'd been scarred by his own parents' traumatic divorce, he might not be able to provide the necessary *emotional* support. He sought and worked towards building a foundation of stability in each of his serious relationships, but ultimately he messed things up.

He continued to find satisfaction in his work. When he was offered *Don Juan DeMarco*, Johnny must have wondered how many ways he could vary a character whose psyche is tilted off

Ed Wood (1994)

center. This film, however, came with major leverage. Johnny was paired with movie giant Marlon Brando.

The creative concept of *Don Juan DeMarco* was as eccentric as both its leading players, based as it was on a screenplay by television-director-turned-schoolteacher-turned-clinical-psychologist-turned-writer Jeremy Leven.

> The film tells the story of a man in love (played by Johnny) whose own passions are so great that he imagines himself as Don Juan, the world's greatest lover. He intends to enjoy the sensual and sexual pleasures of one last conquest before committing suicide. The object of his desire is the one woman he can never have.

Because Johnny's character clearly lives in a fantasy world, after his aborted suicide attempt he begins attending sessions with psychiatrist Dr. Mickler (Brando). Mickler, whose own relationship with his wife (Faye Dunaway) is deteriorating, gradually comes to embrace, if not believe, DeMarco's grandiose tales, and in them finds surprising answers to his own marital problems.

Johnny had worked with co-star Faye Dunaway before in *Arizona Dream* and respected her talent and professionalism, even though she had a notorious reputation for on-set displays of temperament. So how did Johnny react to Marlon Brando, who was reportedly a much more difficult and demanding performer?

Johnny said, "I was really nervous when I drove up to his place on Mulholland Drive. How could you not be overwhelmed at meeting a man who'd done all the incredible things Brando had done in his career? But when Marlon met me at the door and said, 'Hello,' I instantly realized that this movie legend was really just a great, wonderful guy."

Despite Brando's reputation as a moody recluse, while shooting *Don Juan DeMarco*, he let it be known to cast and crew that the door to his trailer was always open, helping to set the mood for a happy shoot.

> **"It was tremendously exciting,"
> Johnny said, "working with Marlon
> and Faye. It was a privilege to work
> alongside them...and learn."**

Johnny had indeed learned much over the short span of his movie career. He'd been honored with numerous acting nominations and critical accolades. But it must have been especially gratifying for the "reluctant superstar" to read Derek Malcom's review of *Don Juan DeMarco*, where he writes: "Johnny Depp stands up to Brando as the best young actor in Hollywood."

This was the first of many critical raves for the film in which Johnny's talents were highlighted over the work of his more celebrated co-stars.

Don Juan DeMarco was released on April 7, 1995, and the movie eventually raked in $22,032,635—high for recent Johnny Depp films, but less than what *Benny & Joon* had earned.

It seemed as though Johnny's relationship with Kate Moss was garnering more (unwanted) public attention than his recent movies. It was reported that their romance had grown increasingly tempestuous. Kate Moss perhaps best explained the true state of their relationship when she was interviewed on *Entertainment Tonight*. In answer to a question about an impending marriage, Kate very simply replied, "Johnny's my boyfriend, that's all. We're not getting married."

They were frequently breaking up and making up. When asked about their splits,

In answer to a question about an impending marriage, Kate very simply replied, "Johnny's my boyfriend, that's all. We're not getting married."

Johnny, as usual, blamed himself. Whether or not he was just being cavalier, Johnny had a penchant for getting into trouble. Often he just happened to be in the wrong place at the wrong time, pissing off the wrong people.

One such incident occurred when Johnny was harassed by an overzealous security guard who demanded that Johnny move his pickup truck, which he'd pulled over to the side of the road in order to light a cigarette. Johnny responded with a wisecrack that the guard did not find amusing, and when Johnny defiantly ignored further orders to remove his vehicle, the guard threatened to call the police. Finally, finding the whole ordeal both irritating and ridiculous, and knowing full well that it would be *he* who would receive the brunt of bad publicity, Johnny drove away.

Johnny had another unfortunate run-in with the authorities—in this instance with a police officer—when he was stopped for, of all things, jaywalking. Johnny was naïve to the seriousness of the violation in Beverly Hills, and again his passion for smoking provided the catalyst for confrontation. As the officer wrote out the citation, Johnny casually lit up a cigarette. The cop demanded Johnny put out his cigarette, and when he refused, the cop twisted Johnny's wrist until he dropped the cigarette. The gung-ho cop and his partner handcuffed Johnny and carted him off to a holding cell for a few hours.

Photographs of a sloppily dressed, unkempt, manacled Johnny Depp were snapped by photographers and then plastered across the front pages of newspapers and tabloids. Johnny thought the actions of the arresting officers were extreme and unnecessary, and he later said, "I've known some Nazi cops who've seen way too many episodes of *Starsky and Hutch*."

Johnny had another unfortunate run-in with the authorities—in this instance with a police officer—when he was stopped for, of all things, jaywalking.

If traffic violations and jaywalking had been the extent of Johnny's controversial public behavior, he might have avoided the relentless press scrutiny that continues to pursue him (at least in the U.S.) to this day. But Johnny involved himself in other incidents that had more serious ramifications.

The most notorious occurred when he was on a publicity tour for *Ed Wood* and had checked into the Mark Hotel in New York. The official version states that on September 13, 1994, at approximately 5:00 AM, hotel security guard Jim Keegan was summoned to Suite 1410, responding to a guest's complaint that a loud commotion was going on inside the room. Kate Moss had arrived earlier to accompany Johnny on his press junket, and sources at the scene hinted that the disturbance was caused by a fight between the two.

At any rate, Keegan, who apparently harbored resentment towards Johnny, based partly on Johnny's casual late-night comings and goings, along with his sloppy style of dress, ordered the actor to depart the hotel immediately or he'd call the police. Johnny apologized and offered to pay for any damage, but Keegan insisted that he leave without delay. It was 5:00 AM, and Johnny couldn't see any reason why he shouldn't check out at a more reasonable hour.

Keegan made good on his promise, and three officers from the 19th Division of the NYC Police Department escorted Johnny in handcuffs from the Mark Hotel. He was taken to the precinct and placed in a holding cell. Although Kate was not arrested, she immediately vacated Suite 1410 and checked into a room at the Royalton Hotel. Johnny's only comment regarding Kate was: "She's probably really mad at me now."

Johnny was once again front-page news in an embarrassing media scandal. His arrest made headlines, and tabloids offered photographers exorbitant fees for exclusive pictures of Johnny in police custody.

Johnny spent his brief confinement in three different holding cells. He passed most of his time reading Marlon Brando's autobiography *Songs My Mother Taught Me*. Later, after he was released and the book returned to him, Johnny found that many of the pages had been defaced with obscenities directed at him.

Johnny was charged with two counts of criminal mischief. But when he appeared in court the next day, the judge immediately dismissed the charges, ordering Johnny to pay only the damages and to stay out of trouble for six months. Johnny never denied the incident and paid the $9767.12, although the actual damages amounted to just $2000.

"I was just stressed out that night," he later said. "I'm human and I get angry like everyone else."

Of course, not "everyone else" is a world-famous movie star, and every time he stepped out of line, his image was tainted in the press.

Johnny was less concerned about himself than the effect such negative publicity had on his mother and teenage niece and nephew. He also said it was a sad commentary of the times when a celebrity's mischief rated equal news coverage with the U.S. invasion of Haiti.

Yet Johnny's public antics, alleged or otherwise, continued to plague him. Just one

Johnny was once again front-page news in an embarrassing media scandal. His arrest made headlines, and tabloids offered photographers exorbitant fees for exclusive pictures of Johnny in police custody.

night after the Mark Hotel incident, Johnny and some friends were visiting a bar called Babyland when he got into an argument with another patron. Johnny's pals interceded and roughed up the fellow quite badly.

Johnny disputed the next day's *New York Post* headline that read: DEPP, PALS IN EAST VILLAGE BRAWL. Responding to the article's labeling him "Johnny Depp-lorable," Johnny offered his version of the events. He claimed the guy was belligerent and made an obscene remark to him as he walked past him at the bar. Although Johnny openly admitted that his first response was "to go for the guy's throat," he controlled himself, respecting the conditions imposed upon him by the judge.

And Johnny was not allowed a respite from his "bad boy" reputation even when he traveled overseas. He hit the British press when he supposedly had a run-in with a member of the British aristocracy at an underground club called The Globe in London's Notting Hill. The story goes that 27-year-old Jonathan Walpole reached for his drink on the bar and mistakenly lifted Johnny's glass. Walpole then claimed that Johnny aggressively "pulled both my ears very hard." Walpole says that his attempts at reasoning with Johnny—"I explained that ear pulling was simply not the way people greeted one another in England"—resulted in his being jumped upon from behind and his head forced forward onto the floor.

> **Johnny's friends steadfastly deny Walpole's accusations, claiming that his story is at most a fabrication, at the least an utter exaggeration. In any event, nothing ever came of Walpole's allegation.**

Even while malicious print continued to malign Johnny's character, defenders came forward who attested to the little-known fact that Johnny frequently cruised poorer Los Angeles neighborhoods, handing out $20 and even $50 bills.

chapter 7

Dead Man's Curve

Although Johnny had distanced himself from television following his years on *21 Jump Street*, he has made the occasional appearance beyond talk show guest shots intended to promote his latest movie. He appeared at the 1994 Academy Awards to introduce another musical inspiration, Neil Young, whose title track for *Philadelphia* was nominated for an Oscar. Johnny's brief speech was short, simple and dignified, although he later confessed to stage fright.

More personally satisfying to Johnny was when he had the opportunity to read the words of his literary hero Jack Kerouac on a PBS special called *The United States of Poetry*. The piece that Johnny recited, set against a photographic backdrop of a declining America, was both powerful and affecting.

While Johnny perhaps could justify these rare forays into television as a way to pay tribute to those who had influenced him creatively, he also contradicted his artistic sensibilities when he allowed himself to become a commercial property for print ads for the European department store Hermes. He did the ads with the proviso that they would never seen beyond their country of origin.

While such blatant commercialism was never a motivating factor in Johnny's selection of film assignments, he continued to be inundated with lucrative big-budget studio offers. Although the failure of his most recent projects had kept him a few steps behind his contemporaries, when casting considerations were discussed, Johnny's name was usually included in the running with Tom Cruise, Brad Pitt and even Leonardo DiCaprio.

> ...he allowed himself to become a commercial property for print ads for the European department store Hermes. He did the ads with the proviso that they would never seen beyond their country of origin.

As predicted, Leonardo's career was on the fast track thanks to his choice of popular movie roles. Interestingly, it was Johnny Depp who propelled his *What's Eating Gilbert Grape* co-star right into the superstar stratosphere when he refused the role of Jack Dawson in James Cameron's $200 million epic, *Titanic*.

Titanic would go on to win 11 Oscars as well as becoming Hollywood's all-time box office champion, earning a staggering $1 billion worldwide (of which DiCaprio reportedly pocketed $50 million as per his percentage deal).

Instead of enjoying a piece of Hollywood's most profitable pie, Johnny was offered and accepted the lead role in a black-and-white eclectic Western called *Dead Man*. Once again, Johnny based his decision on his desire to work with a director whose films he particularly admired.

Jim Jarmusch had impressed critics with his offbeat independent movies, including *Stranger Than Paradise*, *Down by Law*, *Mystery Train* and *Night on Earth*. While his films had garnered major international awards, neither they nor Jarmusch had achieved mainstream recognition.

Jim and Johnny had been friends for several years, and when he approached Johnny about starring in *Dead Man*, he told the actor that he'd written the part of William Blake especially for him. It was a role rife with eccentricities in a movie as odd as they come, fitting Johnny's criteria perfectly.

William Blake is an accountant who travels into the western frontier to begin employment with a mining firm. On his arrival, he is discouraged to find no job waiting. A rendezvous with a local girl leads to tragedy when the pair is discovered in bed by the girl's boyfriend, a notorious gunslinger. Blake is forced to kill the boyfriend, but is wounded in the exchange of gunfire. He must then leave town when he discovers that the man he killed was the mine owner's son. Later, a Native American named Nobody finds Blake and nurses him back to health. Because Nobody believes that Blake is the reincarnated spirit of the poet William Blake, he becomes the accountant's protector, helping him stay ahead of the posse that is pursuing him.

The movie proved another difficult shoot for both cast and crew. Location filming in both Arizona and Nevada was often arduous; everyone coped with unbearably hot days, high winds and choking dust storms. In the end, the picture was praised for its photography, but panned for its slow-moving and confusing story line.

The film's quirkiness was aided by Jarmusch's decision to pepper the cast with actors well known for their eccentric screen portrayals. Chief among this group was Crispin Glover, the hyperkinetic star of *The River's Edge* and the recent remake of the rat chiller *Willard*. Glover's offscreen behavior has occasionally been as bizarre as his movie roles. The most notorious example was when he delivered a martial arts demonstration on the *David Letterman Show* and got so carried away with his fancy footwork that he was removed from the set.

> It is doubtful that Johnny expected sensational box office with **Dead Man**, but neither could he have predicted the scorn with which the picture was received by critics who attended its premiere at Cannes.

Other cast members, including John Hurt, Gabriel Byrne and Lance Henricksen, have confined their eccentricities to their screen work. A definitely

unique Jarmusch casting choice was Iggy Pop in the role of "Sally" Jenko—undoubtedly Johnny's suggestion.

Perhaps Jarmusch's only concession to the traditional Western was his hiring of genre veteran Robert Mitchum for the part of the industrialist. Mitchum played John Dickson with his typical understated brilliance, but *Dead Man*, sadly, proved to be his swan song.

Johnny and Mitchum got along well, perhaps because they shared personal and professional qualities. Neither had "played it safe" with their careers, accepting roles that they found creatively fulfilling, rather than surrendering to the lure of big box office draws. Of course, Mitchum was also no stranger to bad publicity, having endured press slams involving everything from public drunkenness and fighting to a celebrated marijuana bust.

Johnny later recalled of his legendary co-star, "He was about seven feet tall and in great shape. He was a real tough guy. But a tough guy who had enormous heart."

It is doubtful that Johnny expected sensational box office with *Dead Man*, but neither could he have predicted the scorn with which the picture was received by critics who attended its premiere at Cannes. Many of the French journalists jeered the movie and Jim Jarmusch, with one even turning to the director and calling *Dead Man* "a piece of crap." Jarmusch had been the critics' darling with his previous four films, but he apparently

lost his footing
with *Dead Man*.

In his review of *Dead Man*,
Derek Malcolm of *The
Guardian* summed up the
film's lack of appeal: "What
looks like an intriguing short
story is stretched by Jarmusch into
over two hours of slow burning and
effortful watching."

Johnny defended the movie against
the critical backlash, but he also admitted he was tiring of playing "outcasts and
weirdos." While *Titanic* was setting box
office records throughout the world, *Dead
Man* disappeared into art house showings and
eventually turned up on video.

Agent Tracey Jacobs tried to explain her client's poor
batting average with his choice of projects: "He wants to
be in a commercial movie. It just has to be the right timing
and the right one, that's all."

Johnny felt that the time was right. He watched as contemporaries Keanu Reeves and Leonardo DiCaprio exploded into
megastardom thanks to their participation in blockbuster
action flicks. Johnny decided to take the plunge into the box
office pool.

Nick of Time was an action thriller but with a gimmick. The
movie ran in real time, thus heightening its suspense. Director John Badham decided to shoot the picture in chronologi-
cal order, as opposed to shooting scenes out of sequence and
then editing the pieces into a cohesive format.

Loosely based on the Alfred Hitchcock classic *The Man Who
Knew Too Much*, the film features Johnny as Gene Watson,

Nick of Time (1995)

an accountant whose uneventful life suddenly becomes a nightmare when his young daughter is randomly kidnapped and used as a pawn in a political assassination conspiracy masterminded by Christopher Walken and Roma Maffia. The pair tells Watson that he has 90 minutes to kill the governor of California or else his daughter will be murdered. To remind the audience that the minutes are ticking away for Johnny's character, clocks are always in view.

While Johnny seems a little out of place playing an average "everyman" after his long gallery of eccentrics, he believably conveys the desperation and anguish of his character, winning the support and sympathy of the audience. According to director Badham, Johnny also performed many of his own stunts to add to the realism of the role.

However, acting honors must go to the brilliant Christopher Walken who portrays chilling evil probably better than any other actor today. Although Walken won a Best Supporting Actor Oscar for his work in *The Deer Hunter*, he's never achieved major movie stardom primarily because of his own eclectic choice of projects.

Nick of Time seemed to have all the right ingredients: a compelling story, a competent cast and taut direction from John Badham (*Saturday Night Fever*, *Blue Thunder*), yet the film made a resounding thud at the box office, earning just $8,087,783. Critics also slammed the movie, calling its premise "unbelievable" and its characters "cardboard clichés."

> Roger Ebert wrote in his *Chicago Sun-Times* review: "It's a curious sensation, being able to look at the clocks on the screen to tell how much longer the movie has to run."

Nick of Time enjoyed a more successful life on video, but for Johnny, it was a forgettable experience. And so he was overjoyed when his acting idol Marlon Brando personally called him and asked if Johnny wanted to join him in Ireland and "have a little fun."

The "fun" was a co-starring role in *Divine Rapture*. It was a story line that intrigued Brando because it dealt with a series of miracles occurring in a small Irish community that are somehow connected to the local priest. Johnny was to play the journalist sent to investigate the validity of the claims.

The film was an independent production, and so the budget was tight. Despite his enthusiasm for the project, Brando's fee was set at $4 million, including a $1 million bonus just for signing the contract. Johnny, on the other hand, was so eager to work with Brando again that he took a hefty pay cut.

Unfortunately, problems plagued the production right from the start. After proclaiming that the weather was "glorious" during his eight weeks of pre-production, director Thom Eberhardt watched the climate turn rainy and miserable just as he began filming.

More difficulties arose when the Catholic Church in the person of the Bishop of Cloyne forbade the filmmakers the use of two churches for interior shooting. He proclaimed, "Churches are divine and sacred places; they are not film sets." Furthermore, the Bishop was concerned about how Brando's priest character might be perceived by the Catholic community.

The shooting schedule was slated for eight weeks, but Eberhardt

And so he was over-joyed when his acting idol Marlon Brando personally called him and asked if Johnny wanted to join him in Ireland and "have a little fun."

was left without locations vital to his film. Still, he had little choice but to begin rolling cameras, which he did in early July 1995, using Johnny very little, until finally Eberhardt was forced to "temporarily" halt production on July 17. The reason given was financial difficulties. Apparently the $16 million budget was not as guaranteed as had been promised. Eberhardt was suddenly uncertain whether the French backers would be able to raise all the money. He tried to stay optimistic. He assured his crew and cast, which also included John Hurt and Debra Winger, that the production would resume filming by July 21.

Johnny spent a few days drinking in a local pub with actor Val Kilmer, who had recently broken up with his wife Joanne Whalley. Then Kate Moss arrived in Ireland after completing a modeling assignment in Paris. Perhaps sensing that *Divine Rapture* was a doomed enterprise, Johnny took Kate off on a weekend getaway and did not return to the set.

On July 24, a somber Thom Eberhardt announced to everyone that production on *Divine Rapture* was shutting down permanently. The promised production funds were not forthcoming. Eberhardt was greatly disappointed; he'd just watched seven years of planning go up in smoke. In his anger and frustration, he issued a statement blaming the backers for the project's collapse.

Although Johnny personally hadn't suffered a financial loss, others in the cast and crew were not as lucky. As well, many local businesses would now not be paid for the services and accommodations they had provided the film company. Marlon Brando was the only one to emerge from the wreckage relatively unscathed. He left Ireland with a $1 million paycheck since the contract he'd signed stated his bonus was nonrefundable.

> Perhaps sensing that *Divine Rapture* was a doomed enterprise, Johnny took Kate off on a weekend getaway and did not return to the set.

If a lesson could be learned from the failure of *Divine Rapture*, it was that not even the participation of major stars could guarantee a film would see completion.

Misfortune of another sort occurred with Johnny's next scheduled film. *The Cull* was to begin filming in Scotland immediately after Johnny wrapped *Divine Rapture*. The picture was to be written and directed by Donald Cammell, who was perhaps best known for directing Julie Christie in the 1977 science fiction thriller *Demon Seed*. Once again the production ran into "financial difficulties," only this time the director resolved the problem by blowing his head off with a shotgun.

Francis Ford Coppola considered Johnny for the lead role in his proposed filming of Johnny's favorite book *On the Road* by Jack Kerouac. Although a screenplay was written, the project remains in limbo. This is a missed opportunity that Johnny has ambivalent feelings about. In an interview, Johnny admitted to being both excited yet frightened by the part.

After seeing two promising film projects hit the skids, Johnny now decided to take his career in a new direction. He would become a director.

chapter 8

A "Brave" New World

johnny was no stranger to behind-the-camera work. Back during his *21 Jump Street* days, he had directed two public service announcements: one for a child abuse help line and another for the American Make-A-Wish Foundation. More recently, he had directed some videos for some of his musician friends, including the Red Hot Chili Peppers and Shane MacGowan and the Pogues, and had even helmed an eight-minute anti-drug short called *Banter*. But until now, he really wasn't sure he was ready to tackle a full-length movie.

He realized that he had been fortunate to work with some of the best filmmakers in the business—Oliver Stone, Tim Burton and Jim Jarmusch—and with their encouragement, Johnny decided to shift to the director's chair.

The project that Johnny chose for his directorial debut was *The Brave*, based on the novel *Raphael, Final Days* by Gregory MacDonald. A USC film school student named Aziz Ghazal had written a screenplay under the revamped title, and the script had attracted the attention of both Oliver Stone and Jodie Foster, who was also channeling her creative talents behind the camera. However, after Ghazal killed his wife, daughter and finally himself in a shocking murder-suicide, interest in the project waned.

Eventually, two young producers, Carroll Kemp and Robert Evans Jr. (son of the famous producer), acquired the rights to the book and the screenplay, and the latter found its way into the hands of Johnny's agent, Tracey Jacobs. Jacobs liked what she read and passed it on to her client for his consideration.

Johnny wasn't impressed with the script, which he found ponderous, humorless and cliché-ridden. Yet interestingly, he admitted that the story's theme—*Could you sacrifice your life for love?*—haunted him for days after.

The Brave is the story of a Native American (which instantly appealed to Johnny's Cherokee background) named Raphael who is living with his wife and two children in appalling poverty in a desert community. An alcoholic who has recently been released from jail, Raphael applies for a job that will pay him $50,000, an exorbitant sum that is certain to rescue his family from their miserable life. There's just one catch—he must agree to be murdered in a snuff film.

Indeed, *The Brave* presented a chilling, compelling, if ultimately downbeat scenario. Johnny met with the producers to express his interest in the project, but not just as an actor. He also wanted to rewrite the script and direct the movie. The producers instantly agreed, and Johnny and his brother Dan (credited as D.P. Depp) reworked the screenplay. Once the script was completed, Kemp and Evans shopped it around, hoping to obtain studio backing. Even with Johnny's triple-threat participation, studios were wary of investing in such a dark movie. Johnny and Dan then traveled to the Cannes Film Festival, where the brothers managed to raise an estimated $15 million.

Even before Johnny rolled the cameras for his first scene, he discovered that the creative work was only a small component of the overall task of picture making. He quickly found that his myriad organizational responsibilities were far more exhausting than setting up and photographing the action.

"It's a lot of crap dealing with money, insurance, trade union guys," he later bitterly remarked. "If I direct again, it'll be with just five guys and a 16-mm camera. No more 100-man crews. It's too much to handle."

Even before Johnny rolled the cameras for his first scene, he discovered that the creative work was only a small component of the overall task of picture making.

Despite his complaints, Johnny had committed himself to the project. He had millions of dollars of investors' money bankrolling the movie and a team of professional technicians and players just waiting for him to call "Action!"

> To ease some of his burden, Johnny brought onboard friends, such as Iggy Pop, who arranged the musical score, and professional colleagues with whom he'd developed a comfortable working relationship on past productions.

Arizona Dream director Emir Kusturica called Johnny on the first day of shooting with words of encouragement and invited the novice director to call him if he had any questions or difficulties. Johnny regarded Kusturica's parting words a director's version of the actors' ceremonial kick in the pants: "Don't forget, Johnny, f*** 'em all."

As if Kusturica's encouragement wasn't enough, later that morning an already bone-tired Johnny received a second telephone call from Marlon Brando. Perhaps not surprisingly, Johnny had fashioned one of the principal characters, McCarthy, after his friend Marlon, but hadn't even considered offering him the part because he doubted that Brando would accept, and he didn't want to capitalize on their friendship.

Yet during their conversation, in which Brando spoke sagely about his own directorial experience on *One-Eyed Jacks*, the veteran actor took a particular, if not peculiar, interest in Johnny's movie. One week later, Brando called Johnny again and probed him for character details, mainly pertaining to McCarthy. Finally, Brando bluntly asked Johnny whom he had cast in the role of the wheelchair-bound villain. When Johnny admitted that he was still undecided, Brando replied, "I'm going to play McCarthy."

"I was completely floored," Johnny later admitted. "Marlon's coming and doing this film for me was beyond a dream."

While stories are legion about Marlon Brando's egocentricity, selfishness, excesses and professional misconduct, the other side of the coin, as Johnny discovered, is that Brando is also a generous and compassionate man who values his friendships. Brando understood the pressures Johnny was under, and he behaved like a total pro once he arrived at the Los Angeles warehouse to shoot his first scene. While Johnny strove to maintain a light, rather informal atmosphere given the movie's somber subject matter and his own desire to be liked by his cast and crew, Brando's appearance instantly heightened the professionalism of everyone involved.

Such was Brando's regard for Johnny that he refused to sign a contract for appearing in the movie. Johnny reciprocated by not imposing a rigid filming schedule upon his "star."

The great Brando delivered, giving a performance that exceeded even Johnny's expectations. Brando has never been known to socialize on the set, preferring to retire to his trailer or dressing room between scenes, then reappear before the cameras at the last possible moment to retain his spontaneity; therefore, he put complete trust in Johnny's judgment regarding his best scenes. He also welcomed many lengthy conversations with Johnny where the two would dissect their individual interpretations of the McCarthy character.

What finally appeared on film was quite different from the Depp brothers' screenplay. This is particularly evident in the dialogue between Raphael and McCarthy, which in the movie takes on a more introspective, indeed mystical tone, less explicit in its use of obscenities. Naturally this changes, albeit subtly, the more graphic nature of their individual characterizations as portrayed in the script, becoming most evident in their climactic confrontation.

Johnny himself had no problems with the revising of the script. As he said, "Our screenplay was only meant to be the skeleton of the film. I'd say that 70 percent of what we shot wasn't in the screenplay."

Certainly Brando had much to do with adlibbing the dialogue. He'd never been comfortable memorizing lines, and in his later years, was notorious for either pasting his dialogue onto the foreheads of his fellow actors or having lines read to him through a hidden earphone. However, beyond that, Brando's character as presented in the script is required to spew a litany of foul obscenities at Raphael, cursing him and the whole Native American race. Brando's long and much-publicized support of the plight of the American Indian may have created a dilemma between the actor's art and his moral stance, but the outcome was never in doubt.

Johnny never intended to make *The Brave* an exploitive indictment of the contemporary Native American. But he did say of his movie, "I thought it sort of paralleled what happened to the American Indians 100 or more years ago." To his credit the finished film is not a slur against Native Americans, although few would know. When the film was shown at Cannes in May 1977, two years after its completion, many in attendance booed. (Johnny denies this; he claims that the reception at the screening was respectful and positive.) Thus far, *The Brave* has not been given North American theatrical distribution.

Johnny's friend John Waters was with him and Kate Moss at the Cannes premiere, and he spoke appreciatively of Johnny's work: "He didn't make a commercial movie, which I think is good."

Johnny's response to the critical mauling was simply, "The reviews for *The Brave* were written before the reviewers even saw the movie."

Audiences should in fairness view *The Brave*, for many commended Johnny's direction as well as his performance as Raphael. Brando, of course, is likewise praised for his hissably villainous McCarthy, as is Clarence Williams III, best known as

The Brave proved yet another entry in Johnny Depp's growing list of financial disasters, only this time, even the Cannes critics, who are usually generous in their praise of Johnny's films, completely rejected the movie.

"Linc"oln Hayes on TVs quintessential dated crime drama, *The Mod Squad.*

But the bottom line is that *The Brave* proved yet another entry in Johnny Depp's growing list of financial disasters, only this time, even the Cannes critics, who are usually generous in their praise of Johnny's films, completely rejected the movie.

Johnny also lost a great deal of money that he'd personally put up to cover production costs. Worse, he apparently has even lost access to the movie itself. When ex-love Winona Ryder requested a print for a private showing, Johnny had to admit that the film was locked away in a vault somewhere.

> **Johnny's disappointment had him once more searching for a more commercial venture. He was still choosy in his preferences, but he did find one vehicle that appealed to him. He would play the role of real-life mob infiltrator Joseph Pistone, who became known in underworld circles as _Donnie Brasco_.**

Joe Pistone's career was the stuff of pure gangster movie melo-drama. He was an FBI agent who virtually surrendered his life and identity to become an informant against the powerful Bon-nano crime family. He assumed the cover of "Donnie Brasco" and subtly, yet convincingly, gained the mob's trust. Problems arose, however, when "Donnie" found himself getting too close to some of his targets. He began questioning his conscience, if not his motives, when fellow agents prepared to move in for the sting. "Donnie's" greatest guilt came from his association with a low-level hood named Lefty Ruggiero. Lefty had sponsored "Donnie" into the organization and was slated to be murdered once his bosses discovered that "Donnie" was an FBI plant.

Despite some close calls, Pistone survived his dangerous assign-ment (unlike some of the gangsters who paid the ultimate price for trusting "Donnie," such as Sonny Black, who simply disappeared. Lefty Ruggiero was arrested before he could be assassinated, but he would later die of a long-festering cancer). With a $500,000 bounty on his head, Pistone was immediately retired from active FBI service and placed in the Witness Protection Program. He later wrote a best-selling book titled *Donnie Brasco: My Undercover Life in the Mafia*, which was quickly optioned into a movie given the success of such gangster films as Martin Scorsese's *Goodfellas*.

The producer of the proposed *Donnie Brasco* movie, Louis DiGiaimo, had been a high school buddy of Pistone's. He had dinner with Pistone one night, and after hearing Pistone detail the intricacies and intrigues of his undercover work (those that Joe could reveal), DiGiaimo offered to produce a movie based on Pistone's experiences as detailed in the book. Pistone agreed, but the movie would have to be put on hold until he completed his participation in several high-profile mob trials.

When the trials were finished and the book was finally published four years later in 1989, DiGiaimo obtained the film rights and assigned writer Paul Attanasio the task of condensing Pistone's complex memoirs into a taut two-hour screenplay.

Johnny immersed himself in the double life of Joe Pistone/Donnie Brasco. Joe Pistone was not merely a typewritten character, but a flesh-and-blood human being who suffered intense pressure trying to balance his personal and professional responsibilities. Within the movie's allotted 121-minute running time, Johnny would have to express to the audience the variety of emotions Pistone had been forced to live with for years.

Naturally, Johnny had to spend time with Pistone and his family, absorbing all aspects of the man's character, trying to understand what made him tick, while also hoping to determine what toll the potentially suicidal assignment took on Pistone's wife and children.

"I couldn't figure out what kind of guy he was," Johnny said. "Before I met him, I figured there was no way I was going to like the guy. But what I found was one of the strongest guys I've ever met in my life."

Johnny even accompanied Pistone to the FBI training academy in Quantico, Virginia, where Johnny surprised the former agent with his impressive marksmanship.

"I've been shooting guns since I was a kid," Johnny modestly explained.

Shooting began in Florida in February 1996. Just two months into production, Johnny collapsed. Rumors began surfacing of Johnny's continued drug use and his heavy partying lifestyle. Others closer to the scene suggested that Johnny's intense research into the life of "Donnie Brasco" had precipitated an emotional collapse. The latter explanation seems the most likely, since Johnny was diagnosed with heart palpitations, most probably brought on by stress.

Johnny said, "I put a lot of pressure on myself to make it right for the guy because he deserved it. Hell, he lived it. I just played it."

And Johnny did make it right for Pistone, who said, "Johnny brought a sensitivity to the part that a lot of people don't see in me. There were times when I was watching him do a scene where I'd think, *That's me talking*. Depp's a good actor. What's amazing is that he doesn't seem to put a lot of effort into it, he just does it."

It was generally agreed, however, that the ultimate success of the movie hinged not on Johnny's singular performance, but his character's relationship with Lefty Ruggiero. Fortunately, the production received an additional casting coup when Al Pacino signed on for the latter role.

Pacino has played an amazing array of characters in his 35-year-plus movie career. But he will probably always be best known for his work in gangster roles. He played a reluctant Mafia don (*The Godfather* series), a ruthless Cuban refugee determined to climb his way to the top of the Miami drug trade (*Scarface*), a reformed hood trying to escape his street reputation (*Carlito's Way*) and even a comic mobster caricature (*Dick Tracy*). But Pacino's role in *Donnie Brasco* presented the actor with his most (sym)pathetic addition to his cinematic Rogue's Gallery, by playing a defeated, embittered, cancer-stricken mob castoff.

Pacino is noted as being one of the industry's most intense and focused actors. Fortunately, he found a professional kindred spirit in Johnny. He said of his co-star, "Depp is a lot better actor than he is given credit for."

Johnny, of course, reciprocated by saying, "It's sick the amount of talent Al has."

Donnie Brasco perhaps was not the anticipated gangster block-buster of 1997, but it earned a respectable $41,974,656 domestic gross. Both Johnny and Pacino were considered shoe-ins for Oscar nominations, but for reasons unknown, neither was recognized.

Perhaps the pretend tough-guy persona hung around Johnny a bit longer because shortly after completing the movie, Johnny found himself in an incident with the paparazzi, hurling obscenities across the baggage carousel of the Los Angeles International Airport as a persistent photographer demanded to know where Kate Moss was hiding. And while rumors of a breakup continued to swirl around Johnny and Kate, the two were spotted twirling to high energy disco tunes at the *Donnie Brasco* wrap party.

Johnny's next project was to be **City of Angels**, in which he would play a guardian angel who falls in love with the woman he's assigned to watch over. However, when the romantic fantasy was released, Johnny's buddy Nicolas Cage had assumed the role Johnny had declined, co-starring with Meg Ryan.

Johnny always maintained that one of his prime criteria in selecting a movie role is that it must be a project both he and his family would be proud of. To that end, Johnny's eclectic taste in choosing film properties has often been tantamount to an acrobat performing a high-wire feat without the protection of a safety net. He'd had his few winners, and too many losers, although Johnny saw no reason to apologize for any of his choices.

Given Johnny's artistic preferences, *Fear and Loathing in Las Vegas* seemed a logical choice but a project with obvious offensive qualities. The film was based on the autobiographical writings of Hunter S. Thompson, the self-styled "Doctor of Gonzo Journalism," whose life had previously been portrayed onscreen by Bill Murray in the 1980 commercial dud *Where the Buffalo Roam.*

Fear and Loathing details a Las Vegas weekend enjoyed by Hunter's literary alter ego Raoul Duke when he is assigned to cover a desert motorcycle race. Together with Beverly Hills lawyer Oscar Zeta Acosta, Raoul decides to turn the weekend into a booze-fueled and drug-induced kaleidoscopic adventure, the result of which sums up the story's theme: "Just another freak in the Freak Kingdom."

The movie is filled with cinematic excesses intended to either enthrall or repel the viewer—mostly the latter. Not surprisingly, Jack Nicholson was the first to express an interest in developing

the property, but two young producers, Stephen Nemeth and Harold Bronson, eventually purchased the rights. They assigned British director Alex Cox to the project and moved forward with an almost comical $5 million budget (Johnny's salary on most pictures).

Cox and his writing partner Ted Davies quickly discovered that Thompson was a strange and difficult figure to deal with. Besides his creative eccentricities, Thompson clearly had a substance abuse problem. On a visit to his home to discuss the project, they found Thompson incapable of comprehending even the first three pages of the screenplay. He'd been drinking and even suggested that the three pop some acid.

Yet there remained a continued interest among studio executives to translate *Fear and Loathing* to the big screen. Universal Pictures agreed to increase the budget to $17 million and provide worldwide distribution. This, however, was not how Alex Cox envisioned the project. Finally, both he and Davies bowed out, claiming "artistic differences."

Terry Gilliam of *Monty Python's Flying Circus* fame stepped in to replace Cox. Gilliam, the only American member of that distinctly British comedy troupe, was known mainly for his bizarre visual stylings, which found form in his directorial features *Monty Python and the Holy Grail, Brazil, Time Bandits, Jabberwocky* and *The Fisher King.*

Johnny Depp was not the first choice to play Thompson. Keanu Reeves was initially considered for the role, but his asking price had risen astronomically since his *Speed* triumph. The producers simply could not afford him. Although aware that he was not their first pick, Johnny was thrilled to do the movie. He was an enormous fan of the book and most of Thompson's writing.

"He's one of only two writers who can make me laugh out loud," Johnny said.

Speaking of the book upon which the movie would be based, Johnny added, "What I found most fascinating about *Fear and Loathing in Las Vegas* is that it represents a time and an attitude that just don't exist anymore. It's about the death of the American dream, the death of hope."

Johnny had actually met Thompson back in 1994 while Johnny and Kate Moss were at Aspen for the Christmas holidays. They were sitting in the Woody Creek Tavern when Thompson "burst through the doors, carrying a stun gun in one hand and a cattle prod in the other." His dramatic entrance was strictly intended to shock and offend, as was Thompson's style. After the two were introduced, Thompson invited Johnny and Kate back to his home where the two men built a bomb in the kitchen, and Johnny detonated it into an 80-foot fireball in the backyard.

Johnny and director Gilliam hadn't met previously but admired each other's talents and were eager to work together. Gilliam had already enjoyed a far more successful meeting with Hunter S. Thompson than had Alex Cox, and now wanted to meet with both Johnny and Benicio Del Toro, who would be playing the Zeta Acosta character.

Gilliam had absolutely no concern that Johnny could handle the complexities of Raoul Duke. "I think Johnny is the best actor of his generation," he said. "I don't think

> Thompson invited Johnny and Kate back to his home where the two men built a bomb in the kitchen, and Johnny detonated it into an 80-foot fireball in the backyard.

Fear and Loathing in Las Vegas (1998)

there's anything he can't do. He's very inventive and incredibly hardworking."

Johnny had already accompanied Thompson on a Louisiana reading tour (where he was introduced as Ray, the author's road manager and head of security—which fooled no one). Thompson also requested that Depp move into the his house for four months.

Johnny took up residence in the basement room (known as "the dungeon") of Thompson's isolated Aspen retreat. Within five days, he was already exhausted from the writer's irregular routine. Johnny recalled that Thompson's daily routine began with getting up at 8:00 or 9:00 PM, watching sports or news programs, being fed "breakfast" and vitamins by his assistant, getting around to chatting, then driving into town for drinks and more conversation, before heading back home for a few more hours of talk, then bedtime at about three or four in the afternoon.

However, spending time together not only provided valuable research, but Johnny also formed a close bond with Thompson, which was further advanced by their shared Kentucky roots. Once Johnny had Thompson's approval regarding appearance (including a baldpate, which Thompson himself corrected with razors and a can of shaving foam for Johnny), dress, mannerisms and clipped vocal delivery, Johnny was ready to begin shooting the movie.

Benicio Del Toro, who had already appeared in *The Usual Suspects* and would go on to win a Best Supporting Actor for *Traffic*, also underwent a physical transformation for his role, gaining at least 50 pounds,

to play Zeta Acosta. He also maintained a shaggy, unkempt appearance throughout production.

Sadly, all the hard work of Johnny, Del Toro and Gilliam (along with co-stars Ellen Barkin, Mark Harmon, Cameron Diaz and a pre-*Spiderman* Tobey Maguire) was not met with much critical or box office appreciation. The May 22, 1998, release was not a complete misfire; the film earned $10,562,387, (more than most of Johnny's recent movies, save *Donnie Brasco*), and Johnny was generally accorded good reviews for his performance. But the movie's often-gross subject matter could not really be called "light summer entertainment," especially when competing against such blockbusters as *Godzilla* and *Deep Impact*.

> **Many critics regarded Johnny's impersonation of Thompson as "another of Depp's quirky roles in a career that has studiously avoided the mainstream."**

In spite of their mutual disappointment over the film's lack of appeal, Johnny and Thompson continued to speak with admiration about one another. Johnny regards Thompson as a genius. "I really believe he is one of the greatest minds of the 20th century." For his part, Thompson does not consider Johnny a "waterhead," the author's derogatory term for a person he wouldn't waste time on.

Johnny and director Terry Gilliam expressed an interest in working together again and planned a picture called *The Man Who Killed Don Quixote*. The film went into production in October 2002, but filming was halted following an accident involving one of the lead players and remains an on-again, off-again proposition.

For his next project, Johnny chose another admittedly offbeat role but in a genre with broad audience appeal.

chapter 9

Taking a Depp Into Horror

ilmed before *Fear and Loathing,* but not released until 1999, the innocuously titled *The Astronaut's Wife* offered a premise that Johnny found intriguing. Produced by New Line Cinema (*A Nightmare on Elm Street*) and written and directed by Rand Ravich, the movie was the actor's first all-out horror venture since the Wes Craven classic, with a plot that borrowed elements from some of the most beloved science-fiction potboilers of the 1950s, including the more exploitatively named *I Married a Monster from Outer Space* and *Night of the Blood Beast.*

Johnny plays astronaut Spencer Armacost, who with his partner encounters a weird two-minute anomaly while on a space shuttle mission. Soon after Spencer returns to earth, his wife Jillian (Charlize Theron) begins to suspect there's something odd about her husband. When she later discovers that she is pregnant with twins, she also fears that there is something sinister about her pregnancy because she is suddenly plagued by disturbing dreams. Eventually, she discovers that something horrifying did occur during those missing two minutes in space and that Spencer has become the victim of an otherworldly conspiracy.

Despite New Line's promising advance publicity for the film, *The Astronaut's Wife* is a movie of missed opportunities. Questions are left unanswered, such as: What exactly did happen to the astronaut team during their space exploration? Most frustrating is that the movie builds to a suspenseful crescendo, then cops out with a dissatisfying payoff. Critics almost universally panned the movie and dismissed Johnny's

> "He's a wonderful, instinctive actor. It was amazing to watch him layer on the complexities of his character."

performance with little comment. But his co-star Charlize Theron spoke fondly of his work in the movie: "He's a wonderful, instinctive actor. It was amazing to watch him layer on the complexities of his character."

As for the final box office tally, **The Astronaut's Wife** just barely surpassed **Fear and Loathing**'s take, earning $10,654,581.

After completing *Fear and Loathing in Las Vegas*, Johnny was presented with an offer he couldn't refuse—the opportunity to work with the brilliant yet controversial Roman Polanski in the supernatural thriller *The Ninth Gate*.

It is not difficult to understand Polanski's interest in the macabre. Blessed with artistic genius, yet scarred by personal tragedy, he has dealt with his own demons by probing into the dark recesses of his psyche and creating some of the most disturbing images ever committed to celluloid. Polanski first received international acclaim for *Repulsion*, a movie so relentless in its claustrophobic horror and graphic depiction of a young woman's mental breakdown that even today, 40 years after its release, it remains a harrowing viewing experience. Only a few years later, Polanski directed his masterpiece *Rosemary's Baby*, another chilling exercise in paranoia. Polanski experienced real horror that surpassed anything in his movies when, on the night of August 8, 1969, his beautiful and pregnant wife, actress Sharon Tate, and four others were butchered by members of the infamous Charles Manson "family."

The director then endured his own highly publicized scandal after he was accused of having sexual relations with a minor at the home of his friend and *Chinatown* star Jack Nicholson. To avoid serving jail time, Polanski fled the U.S. to France where he has continued his passion for dark, introspective filmmaking.

The Ninth Gate is not a film that would likely appeal to fans of slice-and-dice horror movies. Although Polanski professes a love for such contemporary horror set pieces as vampires and

demons, he rarely aims for the explicit in his own genre offerings, preferring instead to create an unsettling mood.

Polanski admitted to having Johnny in mind for the lead role from the moment he read the Arturo Pérez-Reverte novel *El Club Dumas*, on which the film is based.

He said, "It's rare to find a good-looking man with Depp's abilities."

Indeed, the film dismissed Johnny's former attributes in favor of his talents. Johnny not only took a cut in salary to work with Polanski, he willingly conceded to the requirements of the character by developing a rumpled, bespectacled appearance and bookish manner.

In the movie, Johnny plays the curiously named Dean Corso, a rare book collector hired by the likewise strangely named Boris Balkan to track down a particular volume that was rumored to be co-authored by Satan and included passages that can summon him.

The film, which co-starred former Broadway *Dracula* Frank Langella as Balkan, was reportedly an intense shoot owing to Polanski's penchant for perfection. There were rumors of dissension between Johnny and Polanski during filming.

While Johnny would not elaborate on their creative disputes, he did admit, "It was not an easy movie to make. Roman knows precisely what he wants. Fortunately, he didn't tell me how to say my lines, otherwise I'd probably be in some French jail."

Polanski, however, was **pleased** with **Johnny's work** on the film. He stated, "The way he played **the role gave** Dean Corso an unexpected color."

Johnny enjoyed the part and had no snobbery about appearing in well-written, challenging horror films. He confessed to having a fascination with the paranormal. On the Nevada shoot for *Dead Man*, for instance, he chose to stay at the Mackay Mansion that was rumored to be haunted by the ghost of a little girl. He even supposedly once encountered an evil-looking spirit while staying at a hotel in London that had formerly been a hospital.

His interest in the world of the weird became manifest when he bought Bela Lugosi's Los Angeles "castle" for a reported $2.3 million. Whether or not Johnny knew it when he purchased the estate, it has been reported that Lugosi's spirit has been seen walking the hallways at night.

While *The Ninth Gate* impressed some critics, it was a financial disaster, earning just $18.5 million on a $30 million investment. For Johnny, however, the movie ultimately proved a rewarding experience. In fact, it would change his life.

★ ✰ ★

chapter 10

paradis Found

ver since he'd first traveled to Paris just to sleep in the bed where Oscar Wilde died, Johnny had always loved France. He frequently attended the Cannes Film Festival and admits that besides having the chance to work with Roman Polanski, his main reason for doing *The Ninth Gate* was its Paris location. He'd actually been thinking about taking up residence in the country for some time, and then serendipity stepped in.

He decided to go out to a lounge with some friends to unwind after a long day of filming. Hardly had he sat down when his eyes were drawn towards a stunning woman sitting at another table. She was French singer, actress and model Vanessa Paradis. Depp asked a friend who knew people at the table to introduce them. After that the two spent the rest of the evening finding out about each other.

Johnny never had to wait long for any of his relationships to become serious, and this was also true with Vanessa. Within a month, the two had rented an apartment together, and a few months later, Vanessa was expecting a baby.

Interestingly, Vanessa's singing career began when she was 14, the same age as Kate Moss was when she was discovered. Paradis became a sensation in France with her rendition of *Joe le taxi*. The success was repeated on pop charts throughout the world, hitting Number One in 14 countries. She was soon approached by movie producers and made her screen debut at 16 in *White Wedding*, for which she won a César Award (the French equivalent of the Oscar) as Best New Actress. She had also appeared in *Elisa*, opposite

French superstar Gérard Depardieu and, at the time she and Johnny's met, was beginning work on the film *The Girl on a Bridge*. She then entered the world of fashion and photography as the new face for Chanel's Coco perfume and the body for Jean-Paul Goude's pictures. But when Johnny first saw her at the bar of the Hôtel Costes, he later admitted he had no idea who she was.

While Johnny's personal life was on an upswing, he quickly found himself involved in yet another unpleasant incident in London, while he was out enjoying a quiet dinner with Vanessa and two friends.

A group of photographers spotted him and stared at them through the restaurant window with cameras ready. Because they were clearly after pictures of Johnny and his pregnant girlfriend, the situation became uncomfortable. Johnny finally asked them politely if just for tonight, they'd leave his party alone. The photographers laughed at him and promised they'd be waiting for them once he and his guests came out. Johnny became so enraged they wouldn't respect his privacy that he grabbed a three-foot piece of board and swung it at them, catching one of the men hard on his hand. The photographers backed away without snapping a single picture.

Johnny, however, found himself escorted to jail by London police for another overnight jail stay. He was released the next morning, but was still upset by the event; not so much by his arrest, but because he had been forced into aggressive action by the insensitivity of the ever-present paparazzi.

Once more, the press had a field day. The next day's headlines screamed: HOLLYWOOD WILD MAN'S NIGHT OF SHAME.

On a happier note, Johnny became a father for the first time on May 27, 1999. When Vanessa gave birth to daughter Lily-Rose Melody Depp, he was beside her throughout the entire delivery, even asking permission to cut the umbilical cord. Later, at home, he participated fully in the feeding, changing and clothing of the baby.

Although Johnny has residences in both Los Angeles (the Bela Lugosi estate) and Paris, he plans to raise his family in France, where he has both an apartment in the city and a country home in the South of France. He appreciates everything the city has to offer, from its culture to the general lifestyle. "It's a different thing in Paris," he explained. "It's more about the work than anything called 'celebrity.'"

After Johnny's often-turbulent experiences with the U.S. and British press, he enjoys a more tranquil rapport with French journalists, who have remained supportive of Johnny's work.

The French further showed their appreciation for Johnny's work when in April 1999 they presented him with a special honor for his contribution to cinema at the annual César Awards. in Paris. Equally as meaningful as the award to Johnny was that Roman Polanski gave the introduction.

France and fatherhood seem to have mellowed Johnny and curbed his past erratic tendencies. His focus is now on his family, and as a husband and dad he has excelled. His notorious all-night partying has been replaced with quainter pleasures, such as

After Johnny's often-turbulent experiences with the U.S. and British press, he enjoys a more tranquil rapport with French journalists, who have remained supportive of Johnny's work.

quiet dinners at home or in intimate restaurants. He takes Lily-Rose out for strolls and can enjoy their special times without the intrusion of the paparazzi.

> **Speaking of his new role as family man, Johnny says, "I never thought of myself as a father, and I didn't plan on becoming one. I really believe that Lily-Rose chose to come to us, rather than Vanessa and I deciding to conceive a child."**

The birth of Lily-Rose also cemented Johnny's decision to raise his daughter in France. "I'll never raise my daughter or any child there [in America]," he has said. "I'd rather be in Europe discussing when the grapes are ripe for picking."

Being away from Los Angeles hasn't diminished Johnny's film opportunities. He now receives many opportunities to work in European features, but his name is still red hot in Hollywood. And, more importantly, his friends haven't forgotten him—friends such as Tim Burton.

chapter 11

A Real "Sleep"er

Tim Burton knew that the hero he was looking for would definitely not have traditional heroic qualities, and so when he sought the right actor to play Constable Ichabod Crane for his upcoming production, *Sleepy Hollow*, he looked no further than Johnny Depp.

Sleepy Hollow was conceived by special effects technician Kevin Yagher, who felt he could make a spooky movie based on the headless horseman legend. Yagher teamed up with writer Andrew Kevin Walker, who was trying to sell a script called *Se7en*. The two decided to collaborate on a story that would combine the literary inspiration, Washington Irving's classic Americana *The Legend of Sleepy Hollow*, with the classically British Hammer horror films of the Fifties and Sixties.

What Yagher and Walker wanted was a movie both frightening and violent, yet stylish and atmospheric. Fortunately, they were able to realize their vision when they secured Tim Burton's directorial talents. Burton, who was a great fan of the early Hammer movies, instantly saw the project as a way to pay tribute to the films that had so influenced him as a youth.

Major changes were made to the source material, including a graphic explanation of the origin of the horseman: a violent Hessian, finally overcome by troops, then murdered and beheaded. The friendly Van Tassel family presented in Irving's story became a dark and brooding clan, harboring their own secrets, and a sinister pall hangs over most of the rest of the community, from minister to magistrate.

...when he sought the right actor to play Constable Ichabod Crane for his upcoming production, **Sleepy Hollow**, he looked no further than Johnny Depp.

The most prominent change, however, was in the character of Ichabod Crane. Instead of a meek, stumbling and rather grotesque-looking schoolteacher, in the film he is shown as a young, attractive police detective who tries to solve the grisly Sleepy Hollow murders using modern scientific forensics equipment.

Yet Constable Crane is as fallible as they come. It quickly becomes apparent that he has no stomach for the more clinically explicit aspects of his work. When he is not wincing in disgust at postmortem atrocities, he simply passes out cold, which he does several times throughout the course of the movie.

Although Burton had no doubt about casting Johnny for the role, Johnny was not so sure. He was attracted to the part and wanted to do it, but *Sleepy Hollow* was a big-budget studio film scheduled for holiday release, and Johnny's recent box office was hardly distinguished. Fortunately, Burton had enough clout to convince Paramount that Johnny was the best actor for the part, and they accepted his decision.

Johnny was delighted to be working with Burton for a third time. As he explained: "I think what we have is as close to an ideal working relationship as you can get."

Burton reciprocated: "It's fun watching Johnny work at different things each time; it gives me a renewed energy. Johnny is willing to try anything, and that's what I love about him."

Johnny admitted that his inspiration for Ichabod Crane was his friend, the late Roddy McDowall, and indeed one can see some subtle McDowall characteristics in his performance. He also watched as many Hammer films as he could find to study the acting techniques of genre veterans Peter Cushing and Christopher Lee (who played an opening cameo as the burgomaster). Both had the ability to make the fantastic seem believable.

As usual, Johnny's preparation paid off with a unique interpretation of a most unlikely hero. Although Crane is quite intelligent in his procedural methods, his personal and physical weaknesses make him a distinctly mismatched opponent against the terrifying ferocity of the horseman. It readily becomes apparent that any attempt by Ichabod to end the horseman's bloody reign is about as futile as trying to stop a tidal wave with a teacup.

To ensure that audiences identified the horseman as the epitome of evil, Burton cast Christopher Walken (complete with filed teeth) in the role. Other parts in the picture were played

Sleepy Hollow (1999)

by Burton regulars Jeffrey Jones, Lisa Marie and Michael Gough (an actor of long standing who perhaps achieved his greatest fame later in life by playing Alfred the butler in the Burton *Batman* films). And Martin Landau appeared in a brief cameo as Van Garrett, the first we see to lose his head. Christina Ricci and Casper Van Dien rounded out the cast as Kristina Van Tassel and her bull-headed, but ultimately heroic beau, Brom Van Brunt.

Sleepy Hollow promised to be an audience hit. When it premiered on November 19, 1999, it generated $38 million at the box office—the biggest opening ever for a Johnny Depp film. And while *Sleepy Hollow* failed to make the top 10 list for the year, it went on to earn $90 million U.S., and more importantly, put Johnny back into the ranks of money-making actors.

To cap off his success, after completing the picture, Johnny was honored with a star on Hollywood's Walk of Fame. He attended the ceremony with Vanessa, his mother and stepfather and his two sisters. While some later criticized Johnny for his eccentric style of dress to receive such an honor, he was not mocking the event and clearly appreciated the tribute, thanking all his fans and supporters who had stuck it out with him.

Once again riding the wave of success, Johnny naturally chose as his next project a film with questionable commercial appeal. *Before Night Falls* was the intriguing true story of Cuban poet Reinaldo Arenas, whose success as a National Book Award-winning author at age 20 was overshadowed by the scandal of his homosexuality. Persecuted by the country that had previously held him in high esteem, Arenas was imprisoned before being exiled from Cuba along with other "undesirables" during the 1980 Mariel departures. He lived the next 10 years in America where, penniless and ravaged by AIDS, he committed suicide in 1990.

Before Night Falls scored an enormous hit both at the 2000 Venice and Toronto International Film Festivals. It went on to garner numerous awards, especially for Spanish actor Javier Bardem, who offered a stunning interpretation of the tragic Arenas. The film, unfortunately, went into limited release, and it failed to score with audiences.

> **Johnny's role in the Julian Schnabel-directed feature was small. He essayed two parts: a lieutenant and Bon Bon, a transvestite who helps Arenas smuggle his writings out of jail. But because his roles amounted to little more than cameos, he was barely mentioned in the reviews.**

His role in the more popular *Chocolat* could also be considered a glorified cameo, since he only appears onscreen for 17 minutes of the film's 121-minute running time. Despite this, his presence in the Lasse Hallström-directed film was a main selling feature—his face and name were prominently featured in the movie's advertising.

Johnny expressed surprise that Hallström insisted on him for the movie because Hallström had also directed *What's Eating Gilbert Grape*, and that picture was not one of Johnny's better experiences.

Before Night Falls scored an enormous hit both at the 2000 Venice and Toronto International Film Festivals.

Chocolat (2000)

"My brain was a little unpleasant on that one," Johnny admitted, "and I just wanted to be out of there."

Chocolat is a simple story, fable-like in its telling, set in the French village of Lansquenet. One day a woman named Vianne (Juliette Binoche) appears in town and opens a confectionery shop that produces candies that almost magically arouse feelings long repressed by the townsfolk. While the nobility regards her as evil, the citizens of Lansquenet rejoice over their newfound freedom of expression and celebrate a renewed joy for life. Vianne has brought happiness to others, but she feels her own life is lacking, until she meets Roux (Depp), the captain of a boatload of roaming Irishmen, with whom she begins a romance.

> As with most fables, **Chocolat** presents a gentle moral. In an interview on the **Today Show**, Johnny explained how he perceived the film's message: "It represents the idea of change and allowing yourself to step outside the confines of your normal everyday life and seek out pleasures, and live a little again. It's a romantic idea that you can live simply—just go and do what you want and live how you want to live without hurting anyone, just taking life how it comes."

Johnny particularly enjoyed playing Roux because the film gave him the rare opportunity to play a true romantic leading man, but more importantly, it allowed him to do his own guitar playing for the first time onscreen.

"I saw Roux as a musical kind of guy, a minstrel who lands his boat in a village, busks for a while, and then moves on," Johnny said.

In addition, Johnny has always liked playing characters with accents. He claimed he based his Irish brogue (in the original Joanne Harris novel, Roux was French) on that of his friend Shane McGowan of The Pogues.

> **Chocolat** not only proved strong at the box office, eventually pulling in $68.2 million, but earned five Academy Award nominations, including one for Best Picture. Although Johnny was denied a Best Supporting Actor nod, co-stars Juliette Binoche, Judi Dench and Alfred Molina were each given a nomination.

The new millennium proved a coup year for Johnny as not only *Chocolat*, but *Before Night Falls* received Academy Award consideration. There was also talk that a third Johnny Depp film might be a contender come Oscar night.

The Man Who Cried was another movie featuring Johnny in a small but important role. He played César, a Gypsy horse trainer who falls in love with Suzie (played by his *Sleepy Hollow* co-star Christina Ricci), a Jewish girl living in Paris just before the Nazi occupation.

The film, directed by Sally Potter and co-starring Cate Blanchett, John Turturro and Harry Dean Stanton, is a beautifully photographed but leisurely paced story that unfolds with minimal dialogue. Christina Ricci delivers a particularly impressive performance in that her

> The new millennium proved a coup year for Johnny as not only *Chocolat*, but *Before Night Falls* received Academy Award consideration.

myriad emotions are basically conveyed with body language and facial expressions.

Even though Johnny's part was brief, he displayed an extreme dedication to his craft by having gold teeth permanently installed to be more believable as a Gypsy.

Unfortunately, *The Man Who Cried* had a June 8, 2001, release date, pitting it against such high-powered summer releases as *Tomb Raider* and *The Mummy Returns*. Predictably, the film made little impact at the box office.

from hell...to the
Caribbean

Prior to filming *The Man Who Cried*, Johnny played the lead in what has become one of his most successful yet controversial films. *Blow,* based on the 1993 book by Bruce Porter, is the true story of George Jung, who became one of the prominent players in North American cocaine trafficking in the 1970s. The book was subtitled *How a Smalltown Boy Made $100 Million with the Medellin Cocaine Cartel and Lost It All*, which accurately sums up the story of one man's rise and fall in the drug world.

George Jung was the son of a hardworking but struggling father whom the boy never intended to emulate. Moving to California in the 1960s with his friend Tuna, George began selling pot to the Manhattan Beach crowd and was soon earning quick and easy money from that illegal enterprise. When arrested for trying to smuggle a shipment of marijuana into Chicago, Jung shared his cell with another ambitious drug peddler, who introduced him to the lucrative cocaine market. Upon their release, the two entered into an alliance with Colombian cocaine king, Pablo Escobar and began exporting their product into the U.S. to the tune of $35 million a year.

According to Jung, he was responsible for about 85 percent of the cocaine supply that entered America. Although he enjoyed wealth and success for a time, his criminal world eventually crumbled when he first lost the $100 million he'd amassed to Panamanian dictator Manuel Noriega. Following a series of setbacks that finally landed him a federal prison term, he will not be eligible for parole until at least 2014.

Directed by Ted Demme, *Blow* echoes Brian De Palma's earlier

Blow (2001)

Scarface in that both films deal with ambitious men drawn by the easy lure of power and big money into the cocaine industry. The difference is that Tony Montana was a work of fiction.

Once again, Johnny embraced the challenge of playing a real person and a man not exactly blessed with admirable qualities. Still, he was adamant about giving an honest portrayal, exploring George Jung's virtues as well as his faults.

"I feel I have a **deep responsibility** to him," Johnny told an interviewer.

Johnny visited George in prison a few times, trying to find something about the man that Johnny could relate to. Finally, he found it.

"It's like when I first started acting and really didn't want to do it. But then the money started rolling in faster than I ever could have imagined. I was suddenly on this kind of rise, and there was no stopping it. That's exactly what happened to George, only the fast money he made came from an illegal enterprise."

Johnny even admitted that he could easily have followed the same road as George Jung. "My prospects weren't great. If I hadn't had my music, I could have wound up like George."

All of Johnny's research and soul-searching resulted in a performance so convincing and real that, by the end of the picture, he has virtually accomplished the impossible by winning the audience's sympathy.

Director Demme admitted, "Johnny was really the only guy I thought of for the role. I needed an actor who takes a lot of chances and who would be able to bite into this story more than other actors might be able to. And Johnny delivered."

Demme wasn't the only one to praise Johnny's acting. George Jung himself said that Johnny was "dead on" in his portrayal.

Not to be overlooked, however, is the strong support Johnny received from Penélope Cruz, Ray Liotta, and most especially—and surprisingly—Paul Reubens (TV's infamous Pee-Wee Herman), who gives a standout performance as the gay ex-marine/hairdresser who becomes George's partner then betrayer.

Blow opened on April 6, 2001, to terrific reviews and a positive box office. It also spawned a popular CD soundtrack that featured an impressive cross-section of tunes representative of the era.

Johnny's next film *From Hell* was a historical drama that explored an intriguing premise. Could the notorious Jack the Ripper murders of 1888 be linked to Buckingham Palace? That is what London detective Inspector Frederick Abberline tries to uncover in the most recent version of the infamous Whitechapel mutilations, directed by Albert and Allen Hughes.

The Hughes brothers based their movie on the graphic novel by Allan Moore and Eddie Campbell and presented their own conclusions to the famous unsolved mystery. While the list of possible suspects ranged from a respected surgeon to a female ripper to *Alice in Wonderland* creator Lewis Carroll, the film proposes an elaborate conspiracy perpetrated by the Freemasons to protect the reputation of the British throne.

Originally, British actor Jude Law was set to play the lead role of Inspector Abberline, but when Steven Spielberg requested him for his sci-fi feature *Artificial Intelligence: AI*, he dropped out of the production, and Johnny replaced him.

All of Johnny's research and soul-searching resulted in a performance so convincing and real that, by the end of the picture, he has virtually accomplished the impossible by winning the audience's sympathy.

Johnny had a longtime fascination for Jack the Ripper, and he jumped at the chance to be in the movie. "I first became familiar with the Ripper murders when I was about seven years old and was watching a documentary on the case. Since then I've read so much that's been written about the Ripper that I don't think I'll have to do much research for the film."

In the movie, Inspector Abberline is a detective who has the uncanny ability to see crimes before they happen and sense who is responsible through dreams and visions. He and his pragmatic partner, Godley (Robbie Coltrane), are called upon by Scotland Yard to assist in their investigation, but complications arise when Abberline begins to fall for one of the Ripper's intended victims, a streetwalker named Mary Kelly (Heather Graham), who may hold the key to the killer's identity.

Johnny's Abberline is a role not unlike his Constable Ichabod Crane in *Sleepy Hollow*, although far more interesting and with more depth. While both characters are tortured by past experiences (Crane by his mother's torture and murder by his father and Abberline by the death of his wife and child), Abberline's is a darker soul, and he possesses little of the comic buffoonery that added a touch of levity to Crane.

Abberline is given an added dimension in that, since the loss of his family, he has become an opium addict (à la Sherlock Holmes), and it is through his drug-induced hallucinations that he receives his frightening premonitions.

The film naturally is a dark tale, heavy with atmosphere in a splendid recreation of the fog-laden and gas-lit Whitechapel district. Once again, the directors were admitted fans of Britain's Hammer Films, and this influence is evident in every frame of the movie, which was filmed in Prague.

Because the mood of the picture was so morbid, Johnny occasionally engaged in some good-natured clowning on the set, which was appreciated by all, according to director Allen Hughes.

While *From Hell* did not achieve the success of *Sleepy Hollow*, the film enjoyed a respectable box office and did not hurt the upward momentum of Johnny's career.

As an illustration of the mercurial nature of the movie industry, Johnny was announced for several pictures that a) were never produced, or b) were cast with other players. Sometimes it is a matter of scheduling conflicts, such as when Tim Burton wanted Johnny to play the astronaut in his *Planet of the Apes* remake, and Johnny had already signed on for *From Hell.* (Mark Wahlberg replaced him in the science-fiction dud.) Often a project is cancelled or put on hold indefinitely. This has happened frequently throughout Johnny's career. In 2000 alone, for example, Johnny was set to star in the biographical drama *Marlowe*, the story of Christopher Marlowe, whom some say assisted Shakespeare in writing his plays.

Johnny was also reportedly being considered for *Ghost Rider*, based on the Marvel Comic superhero. Another film based on the life of Scottish poet Robbie Burns has also apparently not gone past the planning stages. Even a BBC announced re-teaming of Johnny and former love Winona Ryder for a Michelangelo Antonioni-directed project entitled *Just to be Together* has yet to see the light of day. And a project that is still periodically announced as "on" is Terry Gilliam's *The Man Who Killed Don Quixote*. Apparently, there has been a renewed, if speculative interest, in the film since the documentary *Lost in La Mancha*, which details the collapse of

As an illustration of the mercurial nature of the movie industry, Johnny was announced for several pictures that a) were never produced, or b) were cast with other players.

Once Upon a Time in Mexico (2003)

this particular project. A further collaboration between Johnny and Tim Burton, a strange tale called *Geek Love*, has yet to materialize. In the film, Johnny would play a murdering circus freak with flippers instead of feet.

Johnny was initially set to star as game show guru, *Gong Show* host and self-confessed CIA operative Chuck Barris in the movie *Confessions of a Dangerous Mind*, based on Barris' autobiography. The production, however, ran into financial problems, and once these difficulties were finally resolved, Johnny had been replaced by Sam Rockwell in the Barris role, and George Clooney, who was only to have played a CIA recruiter, took over directing chores from Bryan Singer.

There had been talk of Johnny playing eccentric billionaire Howard Hughes in a proposed movie biography. But the movie, *The Aviator*, was made with Leonardo DiCaprio in the role.

Johnny was not too concerned about the collapse of these projects because on April 10, 2002, he became a father for the second time when his son Jack was born in Neuilly, France.

> When asked why he and Vanessa had not yet married, Johnny replied, "Vanessa and I have considered ourselves husband and wife since the day we moved in together. We just haven't gone through the formalities of legalizing our union."

However, he has certainly not ruled out the possibility of some-day exchanging vows with Vanessa, joking, "That'll be up to Lily-Rose. She'll rule our roost."

Soon it was back to work when Johnny was signed for a role in Robert Rodriguez's semi-sequel to his hit film *Desperado*, called *Once Upon a Time in Mexico*. The picture was intended as a trib-ute to the late director Sergio Leone, whose spaghetti Westerns, particularly his magnum opus *Once Upon a Time in the West*, were a major influence on Rodriguez.

Johnny plays a rogue CIA agent named Sands who recruits the guitar-playing killer-for-hire El Mariachi to sabotage an assassination plot against the Mexican president by a corrupt military leader and a ruthless drug kingpin. El Mariachi has been living in virtual isolation since the death of the woman he loved, but agrees to the assignment when he is promised a final showdown with his nemesis Marquez.

While the plot occasionally gets convoluted, the film is loaded with enough explosive action to satisfy genre fans and is cast with many familiar faces, including Antonio Banderas as El Mariachi, Salma Hayek, Mickey Rourke, Willem Dafoe, Rubén Blades, and even Cheech Marin (who, although killed off in the first film, returns in a different role as the barman Belini).

Johnny had such a good time making the movie that, after completing all of his scenes in nine days, he suggested to director Rodriguez that he play the small part of the priest that El Mariachi talks to in the church, using his Marlon Brando impression.

Johnny then returned to commercial action fare in a big way when he portrayed the outrageous buccaneer Captain Jack Sparrow in *Pirates of the Caribbean: The Curse of the Black Pearl.*

Pirate pictures had not been terribly popular either with audiences or critics in recent years (Renny Harlin's *Cutthroat Island*, for example), but *Pirates of the Caribbean* had one major advantage—it was based on a popular Disney theme park attraction. So, in a sense, the movie was pre-sold. But that would be underestimating the entertainment value of the movie itself—part swashbuckler, part supernatural thriller featuring some of the broadest yet most enjoyable acting ever seen onscreen, particularly Geoffrey Rush as the villainous and undead Barbossa.

—part swashbuckler, part supernatural thriller featuring some of the broadest yet most enjoyable acting ever seen onscreen, particularly Geoffrey Rush as the villainous and undead Barbossa.

Pirates of the Caribbean: The Curse of the Black Pearl (2003)

Director Gore Verbinski (whose previous film, the horror smash *The Ring* had earned over $100 million at the domestic box office) rounded out his cast with Orlando Bloom and Keira Knightley as the lovers and Jonathan Pryce as Governor Weatherby Swann.

Pirates of the Caribbean is clearly Johnny's picture. From the moment he makes his inglorious entrance, sailing onscreen in his sinking vessel, Johnny steals the show. He could have easily played the part with the heroic derring-do of an Errol Flynn or Tyrone Power. Instead, he sought a most unlikely inspiration for the role—Rolling Stones guitarist Keith Richards. His characterization is so hilariously over-the-top that it keeps the movie afloat during some of its longer stretches.

The film tells of the adventures of Captain Jack Sparrow, a charming rogue whose idyllic life at sea is interrupted when his nemesis, Captain Barbossa, first steals his ship, the *Black Pearl*, and later attacks the town of Port Royal, kidnapping the Governor's beautiful daughter, Elizabeth Swann, and taking her aboard his ship. Elizabeth's childhood friend, Will Turner, who loves Elizabeth even though she is promised to another, enlists the aid of Jack Sparrow to commandeer the fastest ship in the British fleet, the HMS *Interceptor*, in a gallant attempt to rescue her and recapture the *Black Pearl*. At the same time, Elizabeth's betrothed, the ambitious Commodore Norrington, pursues the duo and their motley crew aboard the HMS *Dauntless*. But Barbossa and his crew are cursed and doomed to live forever as the undead—on each moonlit night, they are transformed into living skeletons. When it is revealed that the curse they carry can be broken only by the shedding of Elizabeth's blood, Jack and Will must battle the undead to save her.

> Needless to say, the film is basically an old seafaring action yarn refurbished with state-of-the-art special effects and an outlandish but appealing story line. Perhaps even more outlandish was the phenomenal success the movie enjoyed. To date, ***Pirates of the Caribbean*** has grossed an estimated $621 million worldwide—more than Johnny's previous 11 movies combined!

Although Captain Jack Sparrow is the primary reason for the film's success, Johnny said that initially some Disney executives were concerned that he was playing the character too flamboyantly. "It was like they were scrutinizing my every movement. Why is he acting like that? Why is he doing that with his hand? But I felt so in tune with this character and so confident that I was doing the right thing that I finally said to them, 'Look, you hired me to do a job. You know what I've done before, so trust me.'"

Their trust in Johnny's judgment paid off. For his offbeat pirate characterization, Johnny won the Screen Actors Guild award, and after 20 years in the business, received his first Academy Award nomination. Although Johnny lost the prize to Sean Penn, who delivered an emotionally powerful performance in *Mystic River*, the nomination was a respectful acknowledgment from the Hollywood community of the expatriate actor's vast and varied career.

Pirates of the Caribbean: The Curse of the Black Pearl (2003)

Naturally, the movie's phenomenal success has prompted a sequel, and Johnny has signed on to reprise his colorful role.

On the surface, Johnny's next movie looked to have strong commercial possibilities. *Secret Window* was based on the Stephen King novella *Secret Window, Secret Garden*, which was featured in the author's best selling *Four Past Midnight* anthology. However, Stephen King's movie adaptations have mostly been hit-and-miss propositions, with more misses (*Dreamcatcher*, for instance) than hits.

Yet, it is also the case that movies based on King's shorter works have generally yielded more positive critical and financial results (**Stand by Me** and **The Shawshank Redemption**). So in that regard, **Secret Window** immediately had the advantage of allowing for a tight story line free of the extraneous material so prevalent in King's weighty volumes.

David Koepp had previously scored both as a screenwriter (*Spiderman* and suspense thriller *The Panic Room*) and director (*The Trigger Effect*). In *Secret Window* he parlayed both talents to successfully streamline King's novella into a 97-minute movie, sacrificing none of the suspense and character development.

Creating believable characters has always been where Johnny has excelled. And once more, as best-selling novelist Mort Rainey, Johnny plays a man plagued with recognizable human vulnerability and neuroses (throughout the film, Rainey is either rumpling his hair or clicking his jaw). Sequestered in a cabin in the woods to work on his latest book, Mort Rainey instead spends up to 16 hours a day sleeping on the sofa as he suffers from a severe case of writer's block brought on by the painful discovery of his wife in bed with another man as well as other problems. To add to his troubles, one day a stranger named John Shooter appears on his doorstep and accuses him of plagiarizing his story. It soon becomes evident that Shooter is a violent and psychotic man, whom Mort tries to placate by promising to obtain an original version of the story that would prove his story was published a year before Shooter's version. Shooter agrees, but sets a time limit of three days, which is when strange things start happening, each incident preventing Mort from receiving the needed manuscript.

> Although *Secret Window* might be compared to King's *The Shining*, the movie dispenses with the supernatural overtones of King's earlier book, leaving instead a tidy, if unsettling psychological thriller, replete with an unexpected climactic plot twist.

Co-starring as the creepy John Shooter is John Turturro, and his scenes with Johnny have just the right amount of tension to keep audiences guessing what their characters' next move will be. Also along for the ride are Maria Bello as the unfaithful wife, Timothy Hutton as her lover and Charles S. Dutton as Mort's detective friend.

Critical reaction to *Secret Window* was far more favorable than that given to most other Stephen King genre adaptations, with special kudos going to Johnny and director David Koepp. But what most excited Koepp, more than even the critical plaudits, was the timing of the picture. Johnny had just scored big in *Pirates of the Caribbean* and was now bona fide box office.

> From box office poison to one of Hollywood's most sought-after leading men, Johnny was suddenly deluged with offers...

"We hired an actor, and we got a movie star!" Koepp enthused.

From box office poison to one of Hollywood's most sought-after leading men, Johnny was suddenly deluged with offers, but again selected only those projects that personally appealed to him. Some interesting Johnny Depp projects await on the horizon. Johnny's next released film will be *The Libertine*, in which he co-stars with the equally talented and eccentric John Malkovich in the story of John Wilmot, the Earl of Rochester, as infamous for his promiscuous habits as he was famous for his poetry. Released for Christmas 2004 is *Finding Neverland*, in which Johnny plays *Peter Pan* author J.M. Barrie. The movie, directed by Marc Forster (*Monster's Ball*), is based on the play *The Man Who Was Peter Pan* and focuses on Barrie's writing of the children's fantasy classic in 19th-century England after he bonded with four fatherless children.

On the production agenda is another film based on a Hunter S. Thompson novel, **The Rum Diary**, in which Johnny will again co-star with **Fear and Loathing** alumnus Benicio del Toro, along with Nick Nolte and Josh Hartnett.

A project Johnny finds particularly appealing is the proposed remake of the 1971 Gene Wilder film *Willie Wonka & the Chocolate Factory*, in which he would play the role of Willy Wonka, with Tim Burton set to direct the movie, which is also based on the book *Charlie and the Chocolate Factory* by Roald Dahl.

Johnny's schedule looks to be filled for some time to come. Whether or not any of these or other future projects will set box office records is debatable, such is the fickle nature of audience taste. But with the cushion the success *Pirates of the Caribbean* and its highly anticipated sequel provide, Johnny can safely afford to take a few risks.

Johnny Depp has charted his own career course and successfully navigated the ebb and flow of triumphs and disappointments. He has never become complacent in his success and takes pride

Secret Window (2004)

in the projects he's chosen, even the failures, because all of his choices were made with artistic integrity.

Johnny remains modest and soft-spoken when questioned about his screen successes and is always generous in pointing out the work of others involved, while often downplaying or overlooking altogether his own contribution to motion picture entertainment: little thing called TALENT.

JOHNNY DEPP FILMOGRAPHY

The Diving Bell and the Butterfly (2006)

Pirates of the Caribbean 2 (2006)

The Rum Diary (2005)

The Corpse Bride (2005)

Charlie and the Chocolate Factory (2005)

Finding Neverland (2004)

The Libertine (2004)

Secret Window (2004)

Once Upon a Time in Mexico (2003)

Pirates of the Caribbean: The Curse of the Black Pearl (2003)

Lost in La Mancha (2002)

From Hell (2001)

Blow (2001)

The Man Who Cried (2001)

Chocolat (2000)

Before Night Falls (2000)

Sleepy Hollow (1999)

The Astronaut's Wife (1999)

The Ninth Gate (1999)

Fear and Loathing in Las Vegas (1998)

The Brave (director) (1997)

Donnie Brasco (1997)

Dead Man (1995)

Don Juan DeMarco (1995)

Nick of Time (1995)

Ed Wood (1994)

Arizona Dream (1993)

Benny & Joon (1993)

What's Eating Gilbert Grape (1993)

Freddy's Dead: The Final Nightmare (1991)

Edward Scissorhands (1990)

Cry-Baby (1990)

21 Jump Street (1987-88)

Platoon (1986)

Private Resort (1985)

A Nightmare on Elm Street (1984)

Notes on Sources

Burton, Tim. *Burton on Burton*. Ed. Mark Salisbury. London: Faber & Faber, 1996.

Goodall, Nigel. *Johnny Depp: The Biography*. London: Blake Publishing, 1999.

Hanke, Ken. *Tim Burton: An Unauthorized Biography of the Filmmaker*. New York: Renaissance Books, 1999.

Heard, Christopher. *Depp*. Toronto: ECW Press, 2001.

STONE WALLACE

Stone Wallace has worked as a professional writer for almost 20 years. His first novel *Child of Demons* was published in 1985, followed by his national bestseller *Blood Moon*. Stone attended Red River College, The National Institute of Broadcasting and Robertson Broadcast Academy, but decided upon pursuing a path as a genre writer following the great success of Stephen King.

With the horror market declining in the late 80s, Stone embarked on other creative ventures, including advertising copywriting and celebrity interviews. His connection with many of the great stars of yesterday has resulted in his writing several books on legendary and contemporary celebrities, including *Johnny Depp, Russell Crowe, George Raft, Dolores Fuller* and an upcoming two-book series on Canadian film legends. In addition, Stone has enjoyed a lifelong interest in the gangsters of the 1920s and 30s and has recently seen his historical reference book *Dustbowl Desperadoes: Gangsters of the Dirty 30s* published by Folklore.

ICON
PRESS

STAR BIOGRAPHIES

Real stars. Real people. The life stories of show business celebrities.

LEONARDO DICAPRIO

by Colin MacLean

This book takes you beyond the screen image of Leonardo DiCaprio to provide a probing look at the serious actor who became the world's most famous movie star. Entertainment journalist Colin MacLean uses personal interviews with DiCaprio, exhaustive research and an intimate knowledge of how the Hollywood system works to chronicle the life of the outgoing kid who grew up poor in East Hollywood and who now commands $20 million a picture.

$7.95 USD/$9.95 CDN • ISBN 1-894864-21-2 • 5.25" x 8.25" • 144 pages

ORLANDO BLOOM

by Peter Boer

Hard to believe now perhaps, but when British actor Orlando Bloom appeared on the silver screen as Legolas in the first of the three *Lord of the Rings* films, he was a virtual unknown in the movie industry. In this readable biography, author Peter Boer details Bloom's rise to success, starting with his humble beginnings as a clay trapper at a Canterbury gun club. The book chronicles Bloom's progression through acting schools in London and the back-breaking accident that changed the course of his life and propelled him on the path to stardom.

$7.95 USD/$9.95 CDN • ISBN 1-894864-18-2 • 5.25" x 8.25" • 144 pages

JULIA ROBERTS

by Colin MacLean

Hollywood's highest paid actress is also a fascinating, complex woman who is already a legend. Entertainment journalist Colin MacLean uses personal interviews and in-depth research to find the enigmatic, intensely insecure but dedicated artist behind the famous megawatt smile.

$7.95 USD/$9.95 CDN • ISBN 1-894864-23-9 • 5.25" x 8.25" • 144 pages

GWYNETH PALTROW

by Glenn Tkach

The daughter of producer Bruce Paltrow and actress Blythe Danner, Gwyneth Paltrow first stepped into the media's white-hot glare during her high-profile relationship with Hollywood hunk Brad Pitt. Now an Oscar winner, a mother, a fashion cover girl and an acclaimed stage actress, Gwyneth Paltrow has managed to fly under the radar of the media and remain an enigmatic and intriguing personality.

$7.95 USD/$9.95 CDN • ISBN 1-894864-24-7 • 5.25" x 8.25" • 144 pages

RUSSELL CROWE

by Stone Wallace

Russell Crowe has displayed a versatility applauded by audiences and critics alike, from his notorious early role as the brutal skinhead Hando in *Romper Stomper* to his astounding portrayal as the brilliant but schizophrenic math genius John Nash in *A Beautiful Mind*. Crowe has been compared to many of the great stars of yesterday: Marlon Brando, James Dean, even Robert Mitchum and Spencer Tracy. As this highly readable biography shows, however, Crowe is very much his own man—onscreen and off.

$7.95 USD/$9.95 CDN • ISBN 1-894864-19-0 • 5.25" x 8.25" • 144 pages

Look for books in the *Star Biographies* series at your local bookseller and newsstand or contact the distributor, Lone Pine Publishing, directly. In the U.S. call 1-800-518-3541. In Canada, call 1-800-661-9017.